GHOSTS OF

Niagara-on-the-Lake

SECOND EDITION

GHOSTS OF

Niagara-on-the-Lake

SECOND EDITION

MARIA DA SILVA
AND ANDREW HIND

DUNDURN
TORONTO

Cover image: shutterstock.com/Christopher Meder
Printer: Webcom

Library and Archives Canada Cataloguing in Publication

Da Silva, Maria, author
    Ghosts of Niagara-on-the-Lake / Maria Da Silva and Andrew Hind.

Previously published: Toronto : Natural Heritage Book, 2009.
Includes bibliographical references.
Issued in print and electronic formats.
ISBN 978-1-4597-4212-3 (softcover).--ISBN 978-1-4597-4213-0 (PDF).--
ISBN 978-1-4597-4214-7 (EPUB)

    1. Ghosts--Ontario--Niagara-on-the-Lake. 2. Haunted places--
Ontario--Niagara-on-the-Lake. 3. Ghost stories, Canadian (English).
I. Hind, Andrew, author II. Title.

BF1472.C3D37 2018   133.109713'38   C2018-901431-8
                                                   C2018-901432-6

1 2 3 4 5   22 21 20 19 18

  Conseil des Arts du Canada   Canada Council for the Arts   Canada ONTARIO ARTS COUNCIL CONSEIL DES ARTS DE L'ONTARIO an Ontario government agency un organisme du gouvernement de l'Ontario

We acknowledge the support of the **Canada Council for the Arts**, which last year invested $153 million to bring the arts to Canadians throughout the country, and the **Ontario Arts Council** for our publishing program. We also acknowledge the financial support of the **Government of Ontario**, through the **Ontario Book Publishing Tax Credit** and the **Ontario Media Development Corporation**, and the **Government of Canada**.

Nous remercions le Conseil des arts du Canada de son soutien. L'an dernier, le Conseil a investi 153 millions de dollars pour mettre de l'art dans la vie des Canadiennes et des Canadiens de tout le pays.

Care has been taken to trace the ownership of copyright material used in this book. The author and the publisher welcome any information enabling them to rectify any references or credits in subsequent editions.

— *J. Kirk Howard, President*

The publisher is not responsible for websites or their content unless they are owned by the publisher.

Printed and bound in Canada.

VISIT US AT

 dundurn.com | 🐦 @dundurnpress | f dundurnpress | 📷 dundurnpress

Dundurn
3 Church Street, Suite 500
Toronto, Ontario, Canada
M5E 1M2

To Amanda,
for making the world a brighter place

CONTENTS

PREFACE

With its historical streets, charming shops, and countless romantic inns, Niagara-on-the-Lake lures vacationers in search of respite and relaxation. But in this historic community, ghosts from the past roam the streets on equal footing with the tourists. *Ghosts of Niagara-on-the-Lake* examines the haunted heritage of this town and its environs, collecting more than fifteen of the most enduring and appealing stories.

We're often asked where the inspiration to write a particular book comes from. Sometimes identifying what attracts us to a topic is a difficult question to answer, but not in this case. Once you visit Niagara-on-the-Lake, you will begin to understand why we decided to write a book about this beautiful community. We had travelled to the Niagara area many times for various reasons and always left feeling there was more to discover, more reasons to return again and again.

Naturally, we are as attracted as the next person to the breathtaking architecture along the main street, the wonderful shopping, and the many tantalizing restaurants. But we were also enthralled by something else; in the midst of all this is a rich and fascinating history that comes with page-turning tales of hardship and heartache, tragedy and triumph. This turbulent history forms a perfect backdrop for ghost stories, and it is difficult to find another place so rich in paranormal activity. It seems that throughout the community there are spectral reminders of the past: a young maiden who has waited two hundred years for her handsome soldier to return to her loving arms, the echoes of roaring cannons that reverberate through time, a doomed ghost ship that sails on without passengers or crew, and a charming tavern inhabited by a dashing officer who sacrificed his life to say goodbye to his beloved.

Our visits to Niagara-on-the-Lake have enriched us with an appreciation and knowledge of the town's history, and through this we have found a connection to the countless lost souls who choose to remain in a community that — as a result of careful preservation of heritage buildings and respect for the past — seems to encourage their stay. Thus was born our latest project, the book you now hold in your hands.

Come and explore this other side of Niagara-on-the-Lake with us!

THE BOOK

Ghosts of Niagara-on-the-Lake is written with several audiences in mind. First, those people who are interested in the paranormal and folklore and for whom tales of spirits and spectres are as much a study as a passion. With these individuals in mind, we sought to ensure the stories collected herein were as factual as is possible in the foggy world of paranormal research. Experiences are presented as told to us, faithfully and without unnecessary embellishment, and their historical foundations have been researched extensively.

That emphasis on accurate and in-depth research will, we hope, be appreciated by the second intended audience, history buffs. Even if they should remain skeptical about whether the past — or at least people from the past — occasionally intrudes upon the modern world, they'll still appreciate the gripping stories from which Niagara-on-the-Lake's haunted tradition springs.

The third audience is comprised of the residents of the Niagara Region. This book offers them a wide range of ghost stories — some chilling, others heartwarming — that take place in their own backyard. Most Niagara-on-the-Lake inhabitants instinctively know their community is among the most haunted in Ontario without actually knowing more than a story or two.

Finally, *Ghosts of Niagara-on-the-Lake* is also for the tourists who come to Niagara on vacations or day trips, to guide them on explorations into the town's haunted heritage. And for those people who may pick up the book in a place far away from Niagara, the book serves as a lure, an invitation to come to this beautiful and historical community, Ontario's one-time capital. Ontario's haunted capital.

Ghosts of Niagara-on-the-Lake has a definite historical slant, as most of the ghost stories are tied to people, places, or events from the community's rich past. But while history plays a key part in relating the tales of spooks and spirits, this is not intended as a history book in the traditional sense. In addition, while many of the haunted locales can be visited today, this book is not a travel guide that comprehensively lists all the attractions in Niagara-on-the-Lake. Instead, it is a selection of pertinent sites, brought to life by gripping and often ghastly tales that are sure to provide a new perspective on the locations featured.

A NOTE ABOUT NAMES

The town of Niagara-on-the-Lake has been known under many guises during its two-hundred-year existence, a bewildering number of names that can leave casual readers scratching their heads. In its early years, it was named Butlersburg (after Lieutenant Colonel John Butler, whose soldiers were among the community's first residents). It then went through a series of name changes that included New Niagara, West Niagara, Lenox, and then Newark (the name selected by Lieutenant Governor John Graves Simcoe, who selected the community to be Upper Canada's first capital). Two years after Simcoe returned to England, the town's name was officially changed to Niagara. It wasn't until the late nineteenth century that Niagara-on-the-Lake surfaced.

To prevent confusion, we refer to the town as Niagara-on-the-Lake throughout this book, regardless of the time period.

INTRODUCTION
HISTORY OF NIAGARA-ON-THE-LAKE

Niagara-on-the-Lake is one of Ontario's oldest communities. It's also one of the province's most haunted. Clearly, the two characteristics are related, so to understand the nature of the ghosts that restlessly prowl the town's darkened streets and lurk within its heritage buildings, a bit about the triumphs and tragedies that comprise the history of Niagara-on-the-Lake must be known.

Even before there was a community where the Niagara River pours into Lake Ontario, there was human inhabitation. The first people to arrive in the region over ten thousand years ago were known as the Paleo-Indians. They were nomadic hunter-gatherers who followed the herds of caribou, muskoxen, mastodon, and deer that roamed the Ice Age landscape. Not a lot survives of these early Indigenous Peoples, except for a few stone tools that have been unearthed in modern times.

The descendants of these prehistoric people in the Niagara Region at the time of the arrival of Europeans were known as the Neutral Nation, so named by Samuel de Champlain because they were peaceful with their neighbouring tribes. Unlike their forebears, the Neutrals were not migratory; instead they embraced agriculture and established permanent villages. The mild climate of Niagara, then as now, allowed for a longer growing season, and as a result they were able to grow corn, beans, squash, berries, and herbs. Their ability to grow quantities of food in addition to hunting, fishing, and gathering enabled the land to support a larger population than elsewhere in Ontario, and as a result, Niagara was its most heavily populated region prior to European settlement.

Unfortunately, when the Europeans came they brought with them diseases, for which Indigenous people had no immunity, and homegrown rivalries that embroiled them in bloody conflicts. The Neutrals, caught between warring factions and struck low by pestilence, suffered unimaginably, and within a span of fifty years their population had been reduced to twelve thousand from a height of forty thousand. Thus weakened, they could muster no defence against the Seneca and were destroyed as a nation by the mid-seventeenth century.[1]

Despite being wiped out, the Neutrals left their mark on the landscape by developing trails that we still use today as the route for many of our modern roads, and by giving the region its enduring name: Niagara.[2] Their sacred burial grounds, many of which have been lost to the mists of time, dot the landscape and are occasionally disturbed by modern development.

More than a century and a half elapsed between the time the Niagara Region was first visited by Europeans and the time of its settlement by pioneers. It fell not to the incumbent English or French to establish farms and homes on the site of Niagara-on-the-Lake, but rather Loyalist refugees fleeing the American Revolution. The American Revolution, which was as much a civil war as it was a war against foreign oppressors (the population bitterly divided between Patriots and Loyalists), ended in 1783 with the Thirteen Colonies gaining their hard-won independence from Britain. Some fifty thousand Americans who remained loyal to King George III found their property confiscated, and were ostracized and unwanted in their homeland. Most families fled the newly formed United States and headed to the British colonies to the north. Many of these refugees, who became known as United Empire Loyalists, settled in the Niagara Region.

At first, Niagara-on-the-Lake was named Butlersburg in honour of war hero and prominent resident, Lieutenant Colonel John Butler.[3]

The little village grew so quickly that by 1791, the community, now known as Newark, was named the capital of the new province of Upper Canada (now Ontario). Newark became a cultured island of civilization within a largely unsettled and backward land, and was the heart of its legal, administrative, and military activity.

Unfortunately, Newark's time in the limelight was fleeting. Under the terms of the 1791 Jay's Treaty, which was intended to establish a border between the United States of America and British North America (Canada), Fort Niagara and the east side of the Niagara River were signed over to the United States. The capital was now within range of American cannons, clearly an unsatisfactory situation. As a result, the Town of York[4] (now Toronto) became the provincial capital. Newark wasn't to remain Newark for long; it became known as Niagara and eventually the now-familiar Niagara-on-the-Lake.

The guns of Fort Niagara loomed over Niagara-on-the-Lake for two decades without incident, and the residents of the prosperous town grew complacent to the potential threat of invasion. That changed suddenly and tragically in 1812 when the United States declared war on Great Britain and promptly began plans to conquer Canada. The war came to Niagara when, on October 13, an American force of five thousand men began to cross the river to the small village of Queenston. The resulting Battle of Queenston Heights was a hard-fought British victory, but it cost the defenders its charismatic and energetic commander, Major General Isaac Brock.[5] Niagara, with Niagara-on-the-Lake at its heart, became the principal battleground for the remainder of the conflict, and soon its soil was soaked with blood.

A lull in the fighting lasted throughout the winter, but on May 25, 1813, an American fleet appeared suddenly at the mouth of the Niagara River. Supported by the guns of Fort Niagara, the warships opened a massive and sustained bombardment on Niagara-on-the-Lake's bastion of military might, Fort George. Red-hot cannonballs and exploding shells soon set the fort's wooden buildings alight, and within an hour every building had been razed to the ground, except for the stone powder magazine, which survives today as the oldest building in Niagara-on-the-Lake.

Two days later, weary British sentries looking out onto the fog-shrouded waters watched a sobering sight unfold: the ghostly image of hundreds of rowboats, each bearing a dozen or more soldiers, heading for the Canadian shore. Niagara was being invaded once more.

The small British garrison, assisted by local militia, fought fiercely to oppose the landing, but were outnumbered ten to one and could not hold back the flood of American soldiers. Inevitably, they were forced to retreat and leave Niagara-on-the-Lake to its fate. The town was occupied, and over the next few days the invaders solidified their control, intending to use Niagara-on-the-Lake as a springboard to the conquest of all of Upper Canada.

A defeat at the Battle of Stoney Creek[6] later in the summer put a halt to these ambitious American plans, however. In fact, the fortunes of war were turning decisively against them so that by the onset of winter, the invaders had little choice but to abandon their gains and retreat back to their side of the Niagara River. Before they left, however, they committed what was widely considered to be the greatest atrocity of the conflict: on December 10, 1813, American soldiers burned the entire town of Niagara-on-the-Lake to the ground and cast its helpless people out into the freezing winter night.

Countless skirmishes and raids, as well as several large battles, marred the Niagara frontier for the remainder of the war, and by the time the

Niagara-on-the-Lake endured the horrors of war during the three years of the War of 1812. Many of the ghosts that haunt the community, including spectral soldiers at a number of locations, date to this troubled period.

conflict ended in 1815, the region had been thoroughly devastated. Newark suffered the greatest of all. Virtually all of its homes and businesses were reduced to piles of smouldering ash, belongings looted or destroyed, people left penniless and emotionally scarred. With the ferocity of the fighting over three long years, the pain and suffering endured by soldier and civilian alike, it's little wonder that the majority of Niagara-on-the-Lake's ghostly residents date back to this era.

But while Niagara-on-the-Lake and its people undoubtedly suffered mightily during the war, they soon rebounded. Demonstrating the fortitude and determination for which pioneers were known, residents rebuilt, better than ever, and within a decade the town was flourishing once more. Niagara-on-the-Lake was the administrative and judicial heart of Lincoln, Dundas, and Wentworth counties; was an important transportation hub and commercial centre; served as a depot from which the rich harvest of tender fruit was shipped by steamer or train to distant markets; and was

The popular Ghost Tours of Niagara offer a glimpse into the haunted history of Fort George, the most haunted location in Niagara-on-the-Lake and a community that may well be the most spectrally active in all of Canada.

a military town, serving both as a garrison to British soldiers and a place where generations of Canadians trained prior to marching off to fight in the Boer War and the two World Wars.

Starting around 1860, Niagara-on-the-Lake also became a thriving tourist attraction, luring people from across Canada and the United States, and as far away as Europe. It remains a popular travel destination to this day. Millions visit Niagara-on-the-Lake every year, following in the footsteps of great historic figures like Laura Secord, Isaac Brock, and John Butler. They come from the world over to enjoy all that Niagara-on-the-Lake has to offer: the rich heritage and vibrant culture, particularly in the form of the Shaw Festival Theatre; the breathtaking beauty; the gentle climate; and the many amenities, including elegant hotels, superb restaurants, exquisite shops, and endless fields of award-winning wineries and lush orchards.

With so much to see and do, visitors can't help but fall in love with Niagara-on-the-Lake, a town described by many poets as being as near to heaven as any community on the face of the earth.

Could it be that some of the countless lingering souls who are believed to walk its streets and inhabit its homes — lost, confused, and not of our time — have mistaken this lovely town for heaven? It's a pleasant thought, and perhaps helps explain why Niagara-on-the-Lake is Ontario's most haunted town.

1
LAURA SECORD HOMESTEAD

The town of Niagara-on-the-Lake is home to some of Canada's most cherished historic shrines, but none is more revered than the homestead of the hero Laura Secord, a humble woman whose legendary wilderness trek two hundred years ago warned the British of an impending American attack and likely saved the nation.

With the exception of this one fleeting moment, Laura Secord's story is not one of glory, but rather of hardship and heartache. Her life, like that of most pioneer settlers in early Ontario, was an almost endless struggle. One would think that upon her death, after ninety-three years of near-constant work and worry, her spirit would have been tired and ready for eternal rest.

Perhaps not. It may be that Laura Secord's spirit still walks through the rooms of her former home. If anyone would be strong-willed enough to resist the pull of the grave it would be Laura, a woman who throughout her troubled life demonstrated unusual persistence and determination.

For the first few years of her marriage to James Secord, Laura lived a comfortable existence. True, she worked hard, but her husband was a relatively successful businessman and their farm was well-established.[1]

That all changed, irrevocably, when the War of 1812 erupted and Niagara became a battlefield soaked in blood and hatred. During the war, the Secords and other colonists of Niagara lived in a state of fear, not quite sure who to trust — many residents had freshly immigrated from America and had questionable loyalties — and were constantly worried about their personal safety and loved ones. They struggled daily to tend and plant crops, care for livestock, and conduct business, despite the disruptions caused by war.

Laura tried to ignore the conflict, to remain aloof from the fighting and the dying. But her hand was forced when a small group of American troops appeared at her door on June 21, 1813, demanding food and shelter for the night. During the course of the meal, Laura overheard the soldiers boasting of their army's plan to surprise the unsuspecting British forces at Beaver Dams in the coming days. It was to be a trap. The Secords realized how important it was to warn the British of the coming attack, but who would take the message? There was no question of James going; he had yet to fully recover from injuries suffered the year before while fighting at the Battle of Queenston Heights.[2] The responsibility fell to Laura.

At four thirty the next morning, well before the sun had even risen above the horizon, she set out. It had rained hard during the night, so the ground was a mire of mud, and even at this early hour the country steamed with humidity, promising to be a stifling day. But Laura was on a desperate mission and wasn't about to let anything — or anyone — stand in her way. To minimize the chance of meeting an American patrol, Laura took roundabout routes and avoided the main roads between villages. This added hours to her walk, and each hour added fresh misery. The heat was oppressive and soon her clothing was soaked with sweat. Her feet ached and blistered. Her eyes blurred from the heat, humidity, and fatigue. Still, she kept moving. Alone and hungry, she summoned all her strength to complete her vital mission.

As the sun set, there was some relief from the heat, but there were still other hazards to contend with: clouds of ravenous mosquitoes, night-prowling animals, and the very real chance that in the darkness she might lose her way or take a painful fall. At one point Laura even lost her shoes in the thick woods, and as a result her feet were soon raw and bleeding, so tender that each step was a fresh definition of agony. Finally, when her strength had been all but sapped from her slender body, Laura came upon a First Nations camp. She had to convince these warriors to let her pass so that she might accomplish her goal. Steeling her nerves, she strode into the firelight. The First Nations people were shocked to see a disheveled white

When the War of 1812 broke out, Queenston had perhaps twenty houses, of which the Secord home would have been one of the finest.

woman stumbling from the forest, and at first were skeptical of her story. But when she explained the urgency, they relented and took her across the fields to the headquarters of Lieutenant James FitzGibbon, commander of British forces in the area.

Armed with her information, the Red Coats and their First Nations allies were able to ambush and soundly defeat the American army at the ensuing Battle of Beaver Dams.[3] But Laura received no recognition for her role in the victory, nor any form of financial reward. The Secord family fortunes never really recovered from the disruption brought about by the war and they struggled most years.[4] Laura's financial woes only got worse when, on February 22, 1841, James — the love of her life and constant companion — died.

A widow at the age of sixty-four, Laura had to quickly put aside her grief and look after her own needs and that of her family. She submitted petition after petition over the ensuing years, but the government refused her petition each time.

Finally, in 1860, Laura Secord received the recognition she deserved. The Prince of Wales, Albert Edward (future King Edward VII), toured Canada that year, and on September 8, stopped in Queenston to pay tribute to the veterans of the War of 1812. After being told of Laura's heroic adventure, he made note that upon his return to England he would arrange a reward for her. He was true to his word. The prince sent Laura £100 as thanks for her bravery. It was to be the only financial compensation Laura Secord ever received for her part in a war that could have ended differently if not for her selfless, courageous journey.

Laura's travels came to an end in 1868 at the age of ninety-three. Upon her death, she was laid to rest alongside her beloved James in Drummond Hill Cemetery. Today, and largely because of the heroics and self-sacrifice she demonstrated during that legendary walk in 1813, the Laura Secord Homestead is among Niagara's most popular historic sites. Each year thousands visit the home in which Laura Secord lived during the greater part of her adult life. According to some, her spirit still dwells on the premises.

Countless strange goings-on in the house over the past three decades do seem to suggest that Laura still inhabits the house. On the second floor, people have reported hearing voices. Not the distinct voices of staff or visitors, but rather otherworldly whisperings that hang in the air like a quiet breeze. People look around, but there's no one there. Others have reported seeing a female ghost in an upstairs bedroom at the foot of a bed. Once, these ghostly manifestations were accompanied by the pitiful moans of an obviously pained man. Interestingly, after Laura's husband had been wounded at the Battle of Queenston Heights he endured a lengthy recuperation in this very room. Psychics have claimed that Laura is a sad spirit, but what troubles her is something of a mystery.

Beth (whose name has been changed at her request) worked for the Niagara Parks Commission some years ago, spending most of her time at the Laura Secord Homestead, where she felt strangely at home. Beth was always the quickest to say there were no such things as ghosts, but her experience at this historic building radically altered her view. Over the course of one particular summer, she had numerous encounters with an unexpected — to say nothing of immaterial — guest.

While Laura Secord's ghost is said to appear as a beautiful young woman, the only known portraits of her are as an elderly woman. Her steely determination is evident in this painting by Mildred Peel.

"My first experience happened early in the morning, just as I was walking into the home," Beth explains. "It was my job to make sure everything was in order for the daily visitors, and I felt it was an important job. After all, many people travelled for miles to visit the place where a heroine who changed history once lived."

No sooner had the young woman crossed the building's threshold that particular day than she began to get a strange feeling, and instinctively knew she was not alone. A cold chill slowly seeped through her body even though it was a hot summer day, and goose bumps formed on her suddenly icy flesh. The now-frightened woman could feel someone's presence, yet she could see no one.

"I called out, but got no answer," Beth continues. "I thought maybe my mind was playing tricks on me as I tried to make sense of what I felt. I started to shake off my fear, at least enough to be able to move again. Slowly, I started to walk further into the home. But no sooner did I begin than I froze to a stop, as I clearly heard footsteps across the room above me."

Terror gripped her like a bony hand and wouldn't let go. She tried to scream but no sound would escape her throat. Her eyes widened with disbelief as a white figure, wearing an old-fashioned floor-length dress, gently floated in front of her. Seconds later — though it seemed like an eternity to the fear-rooted employee — the spectral woman slowly began to fade away.

"After that first incident I continued to occasionally hear strange noises in the house, even though there was never anyone in the building. Sometimes it gave me the chills as I entered the home, but I was never afraid again. I knew whoever this ghost was, she didn't mean any harm."

She was just a lost soul greeting her guests.

Another witness, a guest visiting the site, was in the upstairs bedroom when he was startled to hear the sounds of breaking furniture and smashing crockery coming from downstairs. It was loud and violent, leaving the gentleman convinced that a vandal was ransacking the home. He crept downstairs, easing from step to step, frightened that he might stumble into someone dangerous and filled with venom.

Suddenly, the racket was replaced by a quiet that was almost ominous. Worried that the vandal was aware of his presence, the man took no chances and moved with the stealth of a cat. He was prepared for anything, but not what he found when he peeked around the corner into the kitchen. Expecting to find the floor littered with splintered wood and fragments of pitchers and bowls, instead he was stunned to find the room as orderly and tranquil as it had been when he had passed through a little while before.

The Secord home *had* been ransacked once, but that was over two hundred years earlier when American soldiers passed through in the aftermath of the Battle of Queenston Heights on October 13, 1812. No doubt the experience of watching enemies invade her home, remove personal items, and vandalize the property deeply traumatized Laura. Were the otherworldly sounds experienced by the modern-day visitor a type of echo from this event two hundred years ago, perhaps imprinted upon the building by Laura's feelings of violation? It certainly seems possible.

There is no doubt that for almost forty years Laura poured her blood, sweat, and tears into the home. Several of her children were born there;

she watched helplessly as her eighteen-year-old daughter succumbed to typhus there, dying in bed; and it was there that she nursed her husband's war wounds and eventually, years later, mourned his passing. Laura toiled tirelessly to establish the homestead, and she shouldered all of her husband's household responsibilities during his frequent business trips. The homestead's success was almost entirely the result of her labours. As a result, Laura Secord was intimately connected to the property. If, as many believe, a home has a soul, then this one surely belongs to her.

Perhaps this connection between woman and home prevents Laura from moving on, from accepting that she is no longer its matriarch and must now share it with heritage-hungry tourists.

Sometimes the most innocent-looking dwellings harbour visitors from the other side. Such is the case with the charming Laura Secord Homestead.

2
THE OLDE ANGEL INN

The Olde Angel Inn is an English-style pub located a stone's throw from the main street of Niagara-on-the-Lake. As one of the oldest structures in the community, it offers a glimpse into an age long past — just step through its doors and into its nostalgic interior. The Olde Angel Inn's rooms, with exposed hand-hewn beams and thick plank floors laid in 1815, still echo to the sounds of the British soldiers and townsfolk who gathered here for food and drink two centuries ago.

The inn has survived fire, war, and two centuries of change and now enjoys the reputation of being one of Canada's most haunted properties. Rather than attempt to hide the presence of the resident ghost, the owners embrace it as a means of tapping into the building's rich history. Plaques posted just outside the front door tell of Captain Colin Swayze, a British officer who met a tragic death on the premises and has since taken up permanent residence.[1] Many staff members are more than willing to discuss their own hair-raising experiences with the supernatural, and for anyone who spends a night in the upstairs guest rooms, a certificate of bravery awaits them come dawn.

At the Olde Angel Inn, you're never quite sure whether you've been joined at your table by a spectral patron, or whether that shadow flitting across the wall marks the passing of a wandering ghost. That's part of its undeniable charm.

The Olde Angel Inn is perhaps the most authentic British pub in Ontario. The ambience is greatly enhanced by the chance of an encounter with the spectral Captain Swayze.

Another vital element of the building's charm lies in its long and rich history, which dates back to the late eighteenth century and the very origins of the province of Ontario. The early history of Niagara-on-the-Lake, especially prior to the War of 1812, is murky, but people suggest the inn was built in 1789 as a tavern called the Harmonious Coach House, and for many years was the centre of social activity in the community. Since Niagara-on-the-Lake had been selected as the first capital of Upper Canada (as Ontario was originally called), the Harmonious Coach House hosted many important historical figures, such as: John Graves Simcoe, the first lieutenant governor of the province; Major General Isaac Brock, hero of the War of 1812; the famous explorer Alexander Mackenzie; and Prince Edward, father of the future Queen Victoria.

In 1793, the Provincial Assembly outlawed slavery, one of the first such laws enacted anywhere in the world.[2] The legislators were justifiably proud, and to celebrate their achievement, it is believed that they retired to the Harmonious Coach House that evening for a joyous dinner. But despite such important patrons, most of the inn's clientele consisted of travellers seeking food and shelter and soldiers from nearby Fort George, who were all too eager to part with their meagre pay in exchange for whisky and beer. British officers were occasionally billeted at the inn as well.

In December 1813, during the second year of the War of 1812, Niagara-on-the-Lake was burned to the ground by American forces that had briefly occupied the town.[3] Among the dozens of buildings destroyed was the Harmonious Coach House, of which little more was left than a mound of cinders and blackened bricks.

Shortly after the war ended, an enterprising gentleman named John Ross built a second tavern upon the foundations of the original. With a new structure came a new name: the Angel Inn, in tender reference to Ross's beloved wife who he considered heaven-sent. Ross sold the property to nineteen-year-old Richard Howard in 1826, who, despite his age, proved to be a capable proprietor.[4] The Angel Inn then changed hands many times over the ensuing years, and was occasionally known under other names.[5] It didn't even always serve as an inn. At various times since the 1850s it has acted as a library, an apothecary where a pioneer doctor performed bloodletting, and a house of worship.

But the one thing that has remained consistent throughout the years has been the mournful presence of Captain Swayze, whose relationship with the inn dates back to the year 1813. It was during that year that Swayze, a dashing British officer who had been dispatched to help defend Canada during the War of 1812, found himself enjoying a quiet drink at the Harmonious Coach House when he first laid eyes on Euretta. She was the daughter of the innkeeper, a beautiful young woman who served as a server in the tavern and left in her wake the fluttering hearts of countless patrons. What was it about her that moved Swayze? History doesn't say, but it was enough to make him fall hopelessly and instantly in love with her.

In time, the feeling was reciprocated and the two shared a passionate relationship. Swayze imagined a day when the destructive war ended and he could turn his thoughts from fighting the enemy to establishing a family with the woman he loved. Euretta was all he could think of; her smile haunted his dreams, the aroma of a flower playing upon the breeze reminded him of her scent, and imagining the next time he would feel the warmth of her skin distracted him from daily tasks.

The relationship blossomed throughout the year, and it became painful for the lovers to go a day without seeing one another. Consequently, when in December 1813 the Americans approached Niagara-on-the-Lake in overwhelming numbers and the British called a hasty retreat, the lovestruck pair panicked. How long would it be before they saw each other again? It could be weeks, months, perhaps even years. Captain Swayze had to see Euretta one last time, to etch her angelic face in his memory, and to extract a promise from her that no matter how long it might be before he returned, she would faithfully wait for him. Passion clouded his judgment, so while the British forces were in headlong retreat, the young officer lingered behind. Swayze slipped through the shadows of the eerily quiet town, heading for the inn and the arms of his sweetheart.

Unfortunately, American soldiers caught sight of his unmistakable red uniform just as he entered the building, and a detachment was sent to capture him. Peering from behind a curtained window, Swayze saw the enemy surrounding the building and knew he was trapped. He briefly considered fighting his way out, cutting a route to freedom with his sword, but he quickly put such thoughts aside. There were simply too many soldiers. Swayze realized there was no hope for escape. His only chance was to hide. With American soldiers pounding on the doors, he raced down to the basement and concealed himself inside an empty ale barrel.

The enemy burst into the inn and began tearing it apart, searching for the officer they knew hid somewhere within. Swayze's heart raced as the soldiers made their way down to the basement and began thrusting their bayonets into sacks and barrels. Finally, one of the blades found their mark, piercing through wood and imbedding itself deep into Swayze's chest. He tumbled from his hiding spot, crying out for his beloved, his bloodied hands reaching out for her. Euretta pushed through the throng of enemy soldiers and cradled him in her lap. The last thing Captain Swayze saw as his lifeblood drained from his body was her tear-streaked face, tormented by sadness but still lovely. She looked like an angel welcoming the young man into heaven.

According to legend, Swayze's body was buried in an unmarked grave in the cellar where he died, practically forgotten in the records of Canadian history. Almost, but not quite, for though few noticed when the soldier was laid to rest, the spirit of Captain Swayze would always be sure to remind staff and patron alike that he had loved and lost in this very building.

There is no specific date for the first sighting of the officer's ghost, but it was certainly before the 1820s and just a few years after he was murdered. Since that time, all manner of inexplicable happenings and mysterious phenomenon have been recorded at the Olde Angel Inn. Sometimes these strange things are nothing more than "eerie feelings" that come over staff when they are alone in the building — an indescribable sense that they aren't alone, even though they know there is no one else around. One woman has even been stroked gingerly, almost tenderly, on the face. Did she bear an uncanny resemblance to Swayze's beloved?

The hauntings began when disembodied footsteps interrupted the early morning hours soon after Ross rebuilt the inn. The unexplainable late-night wanderings were soon accompanied by other strange noises — whispered conversation, screams of pain, creaking stairs. The innkeeper was left mystified as to the source of the sounds, but it wasn't long before the culprit was discovered. The cause of the inexplicable nighttime commotion appeared one evening, resplendent in his British officer's uniform, misty in form, wandering the darkened inn as if searching for something, or perhaps someone. Captain Swayze has been there ever since.

The spectral Red Coat is assumed to be responsible for the mysterious bumps and other noises that have been heard throughout the building at various times of day and night, and for mischievous pranks that leave staff members and guests alike perplexed. Many years ago an owner was awakened by a crashing sound outside his bedroom, only to find that the heavy horseshoe he'd nailed to a post had been flung twenty feet away by unseen hands. On other occasions, chairs have been propelled across the room, dishes have rattled noisily in the cupboard, the sounds of fife and drums have been heard emanating from an upstairs bedroom. Even today, it's not uncommon for the building's alarm to go off late at night and for the security company to pick up movement on the motion detectors, yet there is never anyone present to have tripped the sensors.

Historical events may help to explain these hauntings. December 10, 1813, is the most traumatic date in the history of Niagara-on-the-Lake. It was on that date that American Brigadier General John McClure turned the people of the village out of their homes on a frigid winter day and burned down their homes. The people of Newark became refugees in their own country, desperately seeking shelter from the biting cold and lashing winds. British soldiers, from the lowliest private to the highest general, were moved to tears at the suffering of these hapless innocents and enraged by McClure's barbarity.

It was on this emotion-charged anniversary that Ian Russell and Trudy Shearing, founding members of Hamilton-based Ghost Hunt Paranormal, descended upon the Olde Angel Inn for an evening investigation. They reasoned that if the Yankee-hating Captain Swayze were to be unusually active on one particular night of the year, this would be it.

"We were looking not only for the ghost of Captain Swayze but also any energies related to the burning," explains Russell. "We stayed in the General's Quarters, which is reputed to be the most haunted of the guest rooms. We chose that particular room, not only for that reason, but also for the fact it is the largest of the rooms. It has two adjoining bedrooms and a sitting room which gave us ample space to set up our equipment."

It turned out to be a wise decision as they were rewarded with a number of unusual occurrences. They didn't have long to wait, either. After setting up the equipment, Russell and Shearing descended the stairs to enjoy a dinner in the characterful pub. While they dined, their digital recorders captured the sound of boots plodding across their room. Of course, the room was locked in their absence so no one could have been in there.

Later that evening, the team decided to use one of the bedrooms in the General's Quarters as a focal point where they would attempt to make contact with Captain Swayze. "I have read accounts of people coming in with American flags in their room to taunt Captain Swayze to get a response. We never taunt when we are investigating. I feel it's disrespectful to the spirits. I would not taunt Captain Swayze if he was alive.... I'm not going to do it now just because he's dead," says Russell, explaining the methods used that night. "We chose to do something different. We brought in a British flag that we laid out on the bed with our equipment as a trigger object, not to disrespect Captain Swayze but to honour him, hoping to get a response through a positive method."

The tactic seemed to work. Over the course of the evening, the team's REM-POD EMF device was triggered multiple times as something interacted with it. Now, the REM-POD is not a traditional EMF detector because, if you place it beside an electrical source, it will not register readings. Designed specifically for paranormal research, it will ignore such false readings. Instead, it generates its own independent EMF field and will only respond if that independent field is disrupted by another source of energy moving through it — spirit energy. Was the ghost whose footsteps were captured on the audio recording earlier in the evening still wandering around the room in the middle of the night? Perhaps.

More strangeness was to follow. Around 2:00 a.m., when the inn was long-since closed and the village sound asleep, Russell and Shearing heard the sound of something being dragged across the floor of the empty pub. "The dragging noise we heard was very heavy. It sounded like some of the dinner tables downstairs in the pub being moved across the floor. There were other guests staying overnight in at least one of the other rooms, but this was not the sound of someone getting up in the middle of the night to go and get a glass of water," Russell remembers.

When the Ghost Hunt Paranormal team checked out in the morning, the inn's staff asked if they had met Captain Swayze during the night. Russell mentioned the late-night dragging noises and was surprised that they were completely unfazed, shrugging their shoulders and simply saying, "It happens."

That tells you something. When staff members are blasé about the sound of something heavy being dragged across the floor by undead spirits in the middle of the night, you know spectral activity is unusually commonplace there and that the Olde Angel Inn comes by its haunted reputation honestly.

It isn't just paranormal investigators who experience the unexpected at the Olde Angel Inn. Many unsuspecting guests have as well. A married couple and their three young children, all under five years of age, retired to the Olde Angel Inn after an exhausting day at Niagara Falls. "They returned to their rooms and piled their shoes in a heap in one corner of the room," relates Lynne Gill, guest services manager at the Olde Angel Inn. "The children slept in the two beds with one adult in each bed and there was no possibility of them getting up without their parents' knowledge. However, in the morning they awoke to find that all the shoes had been matched up in pairs and lined up along the wall, from smallest to largest!"

Had Captain Swayze, the disciplined military man accustomed to order and uniformity, decided to tidy up the room? There seemed to be no other explanation.

Oftentimes guests staying overnight in the second-floor bedrooms will hear the sounds of a bar in full swing — raucous laughter, muffled conversations, the clinking of glasses — well after the establishment has closed for the night and the staff have gone home. Those brave enough to investigate creep warily down the stairs to find that the noise stops as soon as they draw near and the dining room is empty of revellers.

One young couple, newly married and much in love, chose Niagara-on-the-Lake for their honeymoon destination. On the first night, they stayed at the Olde Angel Inn. "We spent a good deal of time researching the 'haunted history' of the area, as it seemed amusing and added a bit of a thrill to our stay," recalls Jennifer Krutilla.

The young couple didn't want to fall prey to any trickery, so they examined their room extensively, checking the alarm clock, or anything else that looked suspicious to them. Everything looked normal enough. But, after learning of the frequently sighted presence of a ghost in the downstairs washroom area, they decided to make a point of visiting the basement. "My husband didn't notice anything of consequence, but in the ladies room I distinctly saw a shadow move while I was washing my hands. I know I wasn't alone."

Back in their room, the young honeymooners fell asleep around midnight. They were later wakened by an awful racket coming from downstairs. "It sounded like tables being moved and thumped around; things even hit the ceiling directly below us. These noises went on for a good half an hour, thumping and bumping," explains the young bride. The newlyweds remained in bed, unable to sleep but unwilling to venture forth to determine the origins of the disturbance. Finally the racket slowly died down, the way a thunderstorm dies down; the young couple still heard the odd bump and thump continuing on after the main ruckus had stopped. "Let me tell you how scary that was!" she recalls.

In the morning the newlyweds made a point of mentioning the unnerving events to the staff, and were shocked to find out that after the 1:00 a.m. closing there was no one in the inn. In the back of their minds they held to the belief that the sounds of the night before were the result of late-night revellers or employees moving furniture. To think otherwise was to accept the existence of ghosts. The staff was adamant that not one person was in the pub after it closed. "I think this may be as close as I have come to a haunting in my life," she says.[6]

While the barroom definitely has its share of unexplainable phenomenon, the basement is truly the focal point of the inn's ghostly activity. It was here, after all, that Captain Swayze was ruthlessly and needlessly killed. Perhaps the emotional trauma of his final moments ensures that his spirit is most tightly bound to the place of his violent death. Some visitors have felt unnatural, spine-chilling cold spots throughout the inn's basement area, the loud clopping of heavy boots can be heard upon the age-worn stairs, and many people have commented on the eerie ambience of "Swayze's Cellar" — some visitors even pause on its threshold and

Captain Swayze is said to be most active in the basement where he met his tragic demise.

refuse to enter. It's here that Swayze's ghostly apparition is most frequently encountered.

But it wasn't in the basement that the most frightening encounter with the long-dead officer occurred. Rather, it was in the streets outside a decade ago.

The fog, almost without warning, swirled off Lake Ontario that early autumn evening and settled upon the sleepy village. The wind had died; the fog a damp motionless shroud, merged with the twilight. A guest at the inn, an American tourist who had been skeptical of the supernatural stories surrounding the building and had not been afraid to say so, was just returning from his day of exploring the attractions when the gloom settled in. He quickened his pace to reach the sanctuary of the inn. As he approached the door, however, he suddenly felt a sense of malice reaching out for him. His nerves were instantly on edge.

Just then a figure appeared in the fog, faint at first, barely a shadowy outline. The figure glided forward, but the fog showed no sign of parting before it or coiling around its shape as it would a solid object. Instead, the figure seemed to simply pass through the fog, and the tourist was unable to do anything but watch its approach with great apprehension.

No more than a few paces separated the two when the shaken American could finally see the mysterious figure's features. It was a soldier from an era long past, his lifeless eyes staring, his unkempt hair rotting, his mouth opened to speak but making no sound. The figure appeared as if it had just crawled out of some stinking grave. Shocked into action, the tourist bolted for the Olde Angel Inn, only feeling safe once he was through its doors and the tendrils of fog that had followed dissipated like a dissolving ghost by the inner warmth of the building.[7]

One question remains: Was the spirit encountered in the gloom that of the usually benign Captain Swayze, or another of the ghostly legion of fallen soldiers that continues to march through Niagara-on-the-Lake?

The story of Captain Swayze has its roots in violence and murder, leaving an unsettling footnote to the otherwise welcoming Olde Angel Inn. Despite ghostly experiences dating as far back as the 1820s, some people remain skeptical of haunted activity within the historic building, believing that the dark stain of Swayze's murder has been scrubbed clean by the passage of two hundred years. But others know differently — the stain is deeply embedded into the grain of the inn's floorboards, forever tying Swayze's spirit to the building that became his tomb. And yet, despite being caught between two worlds and an aching longing for Euretta, the captain seems content with his lot. Certainly, there are far worse places than the charming Olde Angel Inn to be confined to for all eternity.

3

GHOST SHIP *FOAM*

Dawn. The sky was beginning to show tones of orange, and a veil of fog blurred the expanse of Lake Ontario. The man on shore breathed in deeply the crisp morning air. He heard it first: the creaking of wood out on the water. Moments later he saw something through the fog. At first it was an indistinct shape, but the curtain of grey parted to reveal a small sailing vessel that appeared to be a derelict, abandoned and adrift in the open water. The ship listed badly, its hull rotted and the mast leaning wearily under the weight of tattered sails. Not a soul moved aboard.

Moments later, the fog swallowed the ship once more, pulling her into its dark embrace. The man on shore watched, eyes straining to pierce the veil, waiting patiently for the fog to burn away and allow him to once again see the decrepit vessel. But when at last the morning warmth had chased off the mist, it revealed a lake completely empty. It was as if the ship had silently slipped beneath the waves.

This startled witness was just the latest in a string of individuals going back more than a century to see the phantom vessel, an ageless ship that sails the waters off Niagara-on-the-Lake even though the physical ship has long since gone to its watery grave. Many speculate that the spectral craft might be the *Foam*, a yacht that met a tragic end just offshore in 1874. It certainly makes sense, because ever since she was lost, legends have persisted that these waters were prowled by a vessel with no one at the helm, the rigging tangled with wild knots, and not a single living soul aboard.

July 11, 1874, dawned beautifully. Although high storm clouds were building in the distance, the day was sunny, the lake calm, and the wind moderate. It was an ideal day for sailing, and Robert Henderson and Charles Anderson were determined to take advantage of the fair weather. The products of wealthy Toronto families, the two young men were carefree and, on occasion, careless. Many days and most nights were spent carousing and engaging in youthful antics. This day would be no different. Henderson and Anderson decided to take their yacht, the *Foam*, across Lake Ontario to Niagara-on-the-Lake, where they would drink and dance the night away at the fashionable Queen's Royal Hotel. It wasn't too hard to entice five other friends, each one the son of prominent commercial and banking families, to tag along.[1]

The seven chums eagerly piled aboard the thirty-foot yacht at its dock at the Royal Canadian Yacht Club and made ready for sail. By midmorning, propelled by a light wind, they were pulling out into the placid, sun-dappled waters of Lake Ontario. Later, the crew of a passing schooner, the *John J. Hall*, reported that the mood on board the *Foam* was light-hearted, the young sailors singing in high spirits, no doubt anticipating a night of partying. They were blissfully unaware of the disaster that loomed ahead.

Late in the afternoon, a shadow crossed the lake. The sunlight turned dull and the temperature dropped rapidly, chilling the crew. Under darkening skies and failing light, with white-capped waves forming on the lake, the *Foam* found herself short of her destination. Another yacht nearby, the *Ripple*, steered a westerly course, seeking to ride out the storm in the shelter of Port Dalhousie. The young men aboard the *Foam* would have been wise to follow suit, but instead they carried on and put faith in the seaworthiness of their vessel to carry them through to safety.

It was a fatal mistake. Many experienced sailors were of the opinion that the *Foam* was "unsafe for open lake navigation," claiming she was a "skimming fish" subject to swamping.[2] Worse, they pointed out that Anderson and Henderson had committed the most cardinal of sins in a mariner's eyes: they had painted over the yachts original name, *John Powers*, and given her a new moniker. To do that was to invoke a curse and invite disaster. Anderson and Henderson escaped misfortune for a while, but there was

A yacht sailing near Niagara-on-the-Lake. The ghost ship *Foam* is said to cruise these waters still, the souls of five young sailors trapped within her hold.

no evading it forever. In the gathering dusk of July 11, 1874, misfortune finally caught up to them.

Pounded by waves and scourged by winds, the tiny *Foam* was tossed about and her rigging blown away. The young fellows aboard were powerless; they could do nothing but hold on and pray as they were driven toward the dangerous shoal located five kilometres offshore, where the strong current of the Niagara River merges with the lake to create an area of roiling, unpredictable water. The choppy waves drove the *Foam* hard onto the dangerous shoal. Moments later a massive wave crashed over the trapped craft from the stern, engulfing the cabin and filling the hold, dragging her off the shoal and out into the depths once more where she was pulled down to a watery grave.

It wasn't until the next morning that anyone noticed the absence of the *Foam* and her crew of seven. News of the disappearance was telegraphed to ports around the lake, and almost immediately ships were racing for the area of her last sighting. The doomed yacht was eventually located and raised. Salvagers were stunned at what they found. Five of the young sailors were found in their cabins, "fast in their eternal sleep" (of the other two, nothing was initially found, as they had been carried away on the tide). It was shocking. No one could explain why, in their terror-filled final moments, the young men would return to their bunks to await their fate. And why were they found in such a peaceful state when drowning is one of the most terrifying, torturous ways to perish? The answer to this mystery and the details of the final moments aboard the *Foam* is known to no one but the waves and the seagulls.[3]

In the years that followed, people began to report that they had seen a battered and listing vessel floating lifelessly off the shores of Niagara-on-the-Lake. The vision is clear, and witnesses have been fascinated by her sudden appearance, followed by an equally sudden disappearance as the spectral vessel becomes somewhat misty and then, starting with the bow, fades away. This vessel's appearance is attended by a distinctly ominous sensation that leaves witnesses convinced the dark, waterlogged hold of the creaking yacht is now home to restless spirits and nameless terrors. One report even claimed the boat left a wake of roiling fog, sinister grey and thick, like mist escaping from a grave.

While the tragedy of the *Foam* is a distinctly Canadian story, it has left a mark on the United States as well. Supernatural waves lap up against the American shores of Lake Ontario and the Niagara River, bringing with them restless spirits from the maritime disaster. The following frightful tale was brought to our attention, and may be tied to the legendary ghost ship of Niagara-on-the-Lake.

The sun had just set, the sky became dark and grey with twilight, and the first bats of the night wheeled in the sky above when a man driving along the American side of the Niagara River had the fright of his life. Out of the gathering gloom appeared a figure walking aimlessly down the middle of the road, directly in the car's path. The driver slammed as hard as he could on the brake pedal, causing the tires to squeal in protest, to avoid running the pedestrian down. The car came up just short and yet the figure didn't flinch, but instead just kept walking down the middle of the road, approaching the car in a steady stride. It was as if he hadn't seen the car coming toward him, or didn't realize how close he had come to disaster.

Swallowing hard, his heart pounding in his chest, the driver watched the advancing figure. In the glare of his headlights he could see that the wanderer was soaked to the skin, that his clothes were covered in mud and clung to him, and that his hair was matted with weeds stuck to his head, looking as if he had just crawled out of the lake. The driver was shocked. Who was this man? Had he been in an accident? Did he need help and was there anyone else with him? The mysterious figure shook uncontrollably in the cool evening air and reached out a blue-tinged hand in a silent gesture for help. But as the driver opened his door to offer his assistance the figure began to fade from view, disappearing right in front of his eyes. The suddenness of the vanishing left the driver gripped with intangible, trembling fear. The experience tormented the man long after the ghost had been swallowed up by darkness.

Could the vanishing figure have been one of the two young men from the *Foam* who washed up on the New York shore several weeks after the tragic accident occurred?[4] Does he wander the darkened roadways desperately trying to find his way home to gain a sense of closure?

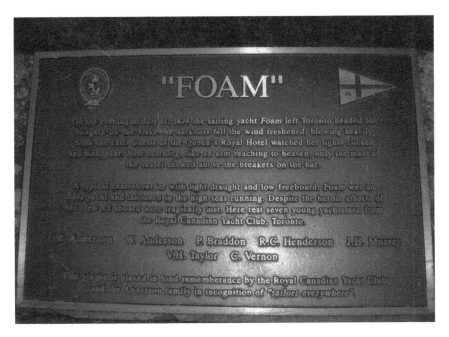

The Royal Canadian Yacht Club erected this plaque in St. Mark's Cemetery in memory of the 1874 maritime disaster. Some say the ghosts of the victims linger in the graveyard.

It has been 175 years and the cruise, which began with laughter and revelry and ended in tragedy and terror, still goes on with no end in sight for the doomed ship. The *Foam* tries desperately to reach shore and allow the spirits of seven young men trapped within its hold to disembark. Only then, safe on dry land, will they find the peace they seek.

4

QUEENSTON HEIGHTS

If ghosts are born of the trauma of people's last moments, as many believe, then surely it makes sense for entire companies of ghosts to exist on former battlegrounds. After all, on these bloodstained fields of conflict, hundreds or even thousands of men had their futures ripped away from them in the most traumatic ways imaginable, cutting short lives that had not run their natural course. Though the dead have been buried and the survivors have since marched off their mortal coil, the Battle of Queenston Heights does not rest comfortably within the confines of history books. Not only has the brutal fighting of October 13, 1812, left a solemn impression that can still be felt on the battlefield today, but many people insist the two-hundred-year-old battle occasionally erupts from the past to be re-fought by spectral soldiers among the land of the living.

One individual, walking his dog through the lightly wooded grounds one pre-dawn morning, unwittingly stumbled into the midst of this other-worldly fighting. A gentle breeze passing through the trees created a sooth-ing rustle as the leaves stirred, hinting at a beautiful day to come. Man and dog walked briskly and happily. Suddenly, the wind began to gust, bending trees, and whipping foliage into a frenzy. Moments later, the walker saw what he is certain was the brief, bright flare of muskets lighting up the murky dawn, and in the momentary orange flashes he could make out the grim faces of soldiers in the midst of a life-or-death struggle. The anxious barking of his dog echoed in his head as a wave of wooziness overwhelmed him, and he had to keep his eyes tightly shut to ward off the wave of nausea. Dimly, he registered the sounds of cannons thundering in the distance and rifles being fired. Despite his heavy retching, the nausea persisted.

Almost immediately the din of combat died. It didn't tail off, as one would expect, with the occasional discharge of a weapon or pained moans of the wounded, but rather ended instantly and completely, leaving a deathly silence in its wake. Even the wind had returned to its previous gentle caress. It was as if the entire event hadn't even occurred, except for the lingering sickness that left his head spinning and the fur bristling on his dog's back. Wobbling on shaky legs, the gentleman returned to his car. It would be days before the unnatural nausea had been purged from his body, and weeks before he could muster the courage to return to the restless battlefields of Queenston Heights.[1]

The fighting this early morning walker witnessed was an echo of that which took place over two hundred years ago during the tumultuous first year of the War of 1812. It seems the ghosts of those soldiers who died at the Battle of Queenston Heights want us to never forget their sacrifice. Sadly, few in Canada know much about the circumstances surrounding

Queenston Heights looms in the distance (about two-thirds of a mile away) in this view, c. 1900. This is the view General Brock and his soldiers would have had as they marched toward battle. Many died upon the Heights during the subsequent fighting and their souls are said to linger there.

this bitter fight and why the area is haunted by countless spirits to this day.

In June 1812, the United States, citing British actions on the high seas and its support of hostile First Nations in the northwest, declared war on Great Britain and began planning an invasion of British-held Canada.[2] The War of 1812 started poorly for the Americans, however, with the humiliating loss of Detroit on August 16 to vastly outnumbered British forces under the inspired leadership of Major General Isaac Brock.[3]

With the approach of autumn, the Americans were determined to avenge their earlier defeat and mustered several thousand men along the Niagara River for an attack on Upper Canada (Ontario). Their plan was to cut the province in half and demoralize the enemy, rendering it indefensible to British forces.

The offensive began on October 12 when artillery batteries along the entire length of the Niagara River opened fire on British positions in an attempt to confuse the enemy regarding the actual location of the crossing. At around 3:00 a.m., six hundred American troops groping through the darkness piled into rowboats and pulled out into the river, their destination — the small Canadian village of Queenston and the strategic heights that loomed above it. Queenston Heights dominates the entire region. Part of the Niagara Escarpment, it is a huge rocky ridge rising one hundred metres above the river, and affording anyone who possessed it unmatched observation of the surrounding area and superior artillery positions. The British recognized the key role Queenston Heights played in anchoring their defences and had therefore built a redan (a V-shaped fortification) atop it, housing an eighteen-pound cannon that commanded the river.

This cannon, along with others placed in British outposts along the river, hotly contested the American crossing. Artillery and muskets flashed in the cold drizzle, causing their targets — the enemy soldiers — to cower in the bottom of the boats. But while the invaders suffered heavily from the fire, they persevered and eventually reached the Canadian side of the river, splashing ashore amidst a hail of bullets and with driving rain pelting their faces. But they were unable to advance any farther, the withering artillery and musketry pinning them to the beach head. It looked for a time as if the Americans would be wiped out on the riverbanks, but a small patrol suddenly changed the complexion of the battle. While most of the invaders were hemmed in along the river's edge, a party of sixty men led by Captain John E. Wool managed to move inland and found a treacherously steep path that led to the heights.[4] They managed to climb up, pulling themselves by root and rock, and surprised the British artillerymen manning the redan. With the heights and the deadly eighteen-pound gun in American hands, the tide of battle swung and now the invaders had the upper hand. Soon, hundreds of American soldiers had assembled on the easily defensible Queenston Heights.

Meanwhile, the sound of gunfire carried down river and alerted the men at Fort George six miles away. Major General Isaac Brock, commander of British troops in Upper Canada, dressed hurriedly and rounded up about two hundred reinforcements, which he rushed to the battlefield. Not willing to allow the enemy to consolidate their position, Brock led a desperate counterattack to retake the redan. It was a fateful decision with tragic repercussions.

The general, leading his troops, sword flashing, was clearly visible to the enemy. His bravery was a magnificent sight and an inspiration to his men, but Brock was also a tempting target for enemy shooters. Without warning, an American rifleman emerged from the brush, took careful aim, and fired at the general. Brock was hit in the chest and stumbled, clutching desperately at the wound. He was dead within moments,[5] but the battle raged on, filling the air with the noise of cannonballs and bullets, the clang of swords, and the moans of the wounded and dying.

Brock's successor, Major General Roger Hale Sheaffe,[6] ordered more troops and allied Haudenosaunee warriors to converge on Queenston. At the same time, small detachments of soldiers in Queenston, though vastly outnumbered, doggedly clung to their positions and continued to harass the boats ferrying American men and supplies across the river.

The Haudenosaunee warriors were the first reinforcements on scene. They ascended the heights inland, out of range and sight of the Americans, then began sniping at the enemy from behind the cover of the dense forest. Though few in numbers, they managed to keep the enemy pinned down in an area of open ground close to the heights' riverside cliffs, and as a result the offensive began to lose its momentum. Whooping loudly, they would charge forward and then melt into the forest like ghosts, their war cries

This humble marker demarks the site where Major General Roger Hale Sheaffe led his troops up the escarpment and to victory at the Battle of Queenston Heights. Ghostly soldiers still shuffle up the hillside to this day.

echoing through the woods and unnerving American soldiers. The prospect of meeting the Haudenosaunee in combat made their blood run cold. Their wild imaginations conjured up images of vast hordes of bloodthirsty warriors waiting for the opportunity to spill a man's gut and scalp his head, and no one thought invading Canada was worth that fate.[7] As a result, many of the Americans (militiamen who were not bound to serve outside their state) refused orders to enter the battle.

Meanwhile, Sheaffe had assembled nine hundred men and led them up a steep path onto the heights. Pausing for a moment to allow his men a breath, he then marched them forward, ordered a single volley fired at the shaken Americans, and then charged with bayonets fixed. The soldiers needed no encouragement. To a man they wanted vengeance for the loss of Brock. The Red Coats surged forward — nine hundred hearts burning with revenge. The assault was so determined, so overwhelming in its ferocity that it took less than fifteen minutes for resistance to collapse. Many Americans died by bullet or bayonet. Some fell from the cliffs in a desperate bid for escape and were dashed on the rocks below. A few even managed to

S.E. View of Brock's Monument on Queenston Heights as it appeared May 9th A.D. 1841.

A towering edifice built in 1824, Brock's Monument was designed to honour a fallen hero, but was irreparably damaged in an 1840 explosion orchestrated by anti-British terrorist Benjamin Lett. Perhaps that violence helped unsettle the battlefield. The monument was rebuilt in 1853.

get back to the boats. But most soldiers simply threw down their weapons in surrender. The battle that had started around 3:00 a.m. the night before ended around 3:00 p.m. During twelve hours of fighting, the Americans lost as many as 250 dead (buried where they fell, their graves unmarked and forgotten) and another 925 captured.[8] Losses on the British side amounted to only fourteen dead and seventy-seven wounded.

Memories of that bloody, corpse-strewn battlefield took years to fade. And while it took time for veterans of the fighting to put those tragic and heart-rending days behind them, eventually they succeeded in focusing their energies on the opportunities of the present. They were so successful that today the battle is all but forgotten, kept alive only by those with a passion for history and the restless spirits who relive the firing, bayoneting, clubbing, and dying over and over again. And while Queenston Heights is a picturesque parkland today, it's said that the entire battlefield is littered with lost souls from that bloody day over two hundred years ago.

How many ghostly soldiers are there? Whose flag did they fight under, and why do they remain? No one knows for certain, but these spirits — individually and in company strength — have been appearing for as far back as anyone can remember. Witnesses claim to hear the sound of battle carried upon the breeze; the pitiful moans of wounded and dying men and animals; the roar of cannons, the echo of musketry; the harsh bark of commands; spine-chilling war cries; sabres rattling in their scabbards; and the marching of hundreds of invisible boots in practised unison. Others feel the heavy loss of life weighing down on them, darkening their mood, bringing them to the point of tears. Sometimes this unsettling sensation is accompanied by a stench in the air, a nauseating blend of gunpowder and blood.

It isn't just sounds and sensations that people experience at Queenston Heights. Sometimes the encounter is visual in nature, involving sights that leave the witness's heart frozen somewhere between fear and awe. Some say if you look closely when day gives way to darkness, ghostly soldiers can be seen rising up from the earth and wandering the grounds of Queenston Heights. Other reports suggest the time of day has little bearing on one's chances of having an otherworldly encounter, that apparitions have even been seen during full daylight marching through the parkland, completely oblivious to the living.

Brock's Monument is the centrepiece of Queenston Heights. Major General Isaac Brock is interred beneath the tower, and from the top of its 235-step spiral staircase visitors enjoy a spectacular view of the Niagara Region.

Sometimes the ghostly soldiers spill off the battlefield and over the sides of the escarpment to intrude upon the surrounding lands. One of these rare occurrences took place a few years back when, during an early evening like any other, a young man was driving along York Road. The sun had set and shadows were stretching across the landscape, but he was admiring the charming scenery and in no particular hurry. He slowed the car to take in the many historical homes sitting alongside the road and to marvel at the picturesque Niagara Escarpment that went on for as far as the eye could see.

This young man was familiar with the history of Niagara-on-the-Lake and its tradition of hauntings, but in all the times he had driven this stretch of road not a single thing had occurred to make him believe restless souls walked alongside the area's countless tourists. This evening would be different, however, and would cause him to re-examine his beliefs. He was just coming upon a small, unassuming stone monument that stands beside the road when he saw at least a dozen red-coated soldiers, perhaps even more, marching single file up the escarpment with muskets at hand and ready for battle. Coincidentally, that marker signifies the location where the British army, under the command of General Roger Hale Sheaffe climbed the escarpment to attack the rear of the American army, thus winning the Battle of Queenston Heights.

The young driver couldn't believe his eyes; he could almost see through the soldiers, whose skin, uniforms, and equipment were all a luminescent blue-grey, as if they were the colour of moonlight. The vision lasted mere seconds before the soldiers slowly faded from view as the woods swallowed them up. He didn't know what to think, but was left believing he had just witnessed an echo of a moment in time from over two centuries ago, and that those who fought and spilled their blood here continue to appear because they do not want to be forgotten.

Will the tortured spirits that continue to wage their phantom battle ever agree to a truce and put an end to over two hundred years of fighting? Or is their term of enlistment for all eternity? Only time will tell. But surely these men have done their duty and deserve peace.

5
LAKEFRONT GAZEBO

During the day, Queen's Royal Park and its famous Lakefront Gazebo are among the most beautiful and frequently visited attractions in Niagara-on-the-Lake. Thanks to its unobstructed views out onto the Niagara River and Lake Ontario and the tranquility that surrounds the setting, the park is a popular place for camera-toting tourists and couples seeking to share a few romantic moments. Indeed, it's so picturesque that numerous weddings are held under the gazebo every year.

But at night, things change. The park becomes a place of fear and anxiety. It's amazing how childhood fears stay with you into adult life. The rational mind knows that the shapes and shadows are made by ordinary objects, but many visitors to the park after dark feel a tightness in their chests just the same. The gazebo, so alluring by day, takes on the shape of a cage by night, while tree branches resemble grasping claws and the dark mass of a shrub looks like some crouching animal. And then there's the shadowy woman wading along the water's edge. A shawl is pulled protectively around her body, her head is turned to look out upon the expanse of the lake, and faint sobs play upon the breeze. She leaves no ripples in her wake, and the moonlight passes through her body. How can there be any rational explanation for her?

Such stories might easily be dismissed as the product of overactive imaginations by people familiar with the park's infamous past. In 1983, David

Lakefront Gazebo, where a ghostly woman in eternal torment wanders the shores of Lake Ontario in the fading light of day.

Cronenberg selected the site as a location for his horror film, *The Dead Zone*, based on a Stephen King novel of the same name about a man who awakens from a coma to discover he has psychic abilities that both help and haunt him.[1] The gazebo, which was built specifically for the film and gifted to the town of Niagara-on-the-Lake afterwards, was the scene of cinematic rape and murder.

Some skeptics believe the park's haunted traditions can be traced back to this movie and the power of suggestion it plants in people's minds. Such a rationale might be plausible, except for one thing — the ghost stories surrounding the location predate the film by many years. In fact, they probably go back a century or more, when this very site was the location of the Queen's Royal Hotel, the most splendid hotel in Niagara. When it opened for business in 1868, this hotel set the standard for elegance in Niagara and served as the catalyst for a new age of prosperity for the town.[2]

The Queen's Royal Hotel was the first deluxe hotel in Niagara-on-the-Lake, and guests found themselves in an oasis of luxury in one of the most beautiful locations in the world. It was huge for its time, a four-storey resort known for its excellent service, uniformed bellhops, and fine dining. As Kaye Toye explains, the hotel's location only enhanced its charm: "Wide breezy verandahs supplied ample room for guests to while away their time comfortably in rocking chairs, as they gazed on the placid unpolluted river."[3] And the amenities were first rate, including a beautiful green for lawn bowling, a sandy beach ideal for swimming and boating, world-class tennis courts, and an adjacent golf course on the site of historic Fort Mississauga.[4]

Guests came from all over Canada, Europe, and, especially, the southern United States. Many vacationers would stay at the hotel for weeks in the summer, if not the entire season, and some went so far as to reserve the same room year after year. In the hotel's heyday, four steamers arrived daily with vacationers, the wealthiest of which were always destined for the Queen's Royal. In 1901, the future King George V and Queen Mary enjoyed the hotel's unrivalled hospitality during their Canadian tour.

But Queen's Royal would sit upon its throne as the monarch of Niagara hotels for only fifty years. The First World War naturally caused a downturn in business, but the hotel's owners fervently hoped that with the end of the conflict the summer tourists would return and restore their fortunes. It did not happen. People simply did not come in the numbers the owners imagined. Try as they might, there was no way to balance the books or restore the hotel's faded lustre. By 1925, the Queen's Royal Hotel was bankrupt and sold to new owners, who had no intention of restoring it. First the extensive grounds were sold off, followed shortly by the furniture and fixtures. Finally, in 1930, the once-grand hotel was demolished before a crowd of saddened, teary-eyed locals.

Since then, countless witnesses have reported seeing a woman weeping near or within the gazebo, and before its construction at the water's edge at Queen's Royal Park. The spectral figure appears to be wearing a long white dress with a dark shawl draped over her shoulders to ward off a chill she can no longer feel. Most witnesses agree she's a young woman, certainly not older than thirty, and that her face is a mask of sadness and sorrow. Sometimes the figure just stands there, frozen to one spot, looking intently out upon the waters of Lake Ontario. Other times she paces the shoreline anxiously, her hands gently holding her face as tears of despair stream down her cheeks. When she appears she brings with her an aura of sorrow and despondency that hangs heavily in the air, bringing eyewitnesses to the verge of tears. If anyone approaches the tragic ghost, she simply disappears, leaving the witness confused.

What is this ghostly woman's story? Why is she bound to the water's edge, and what heart-rending event causes her such enduring sadness? History doesn't provide the answers, but a psychic who had an unusually vivid experience at Queen's Royal Park may. "I really don't know where to start," the psychic, a Niagara resident who asked to remain anonymous, told us. "But I'll try to tell the story as best as I can, as it was related to me by the spirit herself. It went something like this":

I was only twenty-two years old and in love with a man who was thirty. We had been trying very hard to start a family, but unfortunately it simply was not happening. I had talked my husband into getting away from the familiar things, to see if a change of scenery would help us with our desire for a family. We decided to spend some time at the Queen's Royal Hotel in Niagara-on-the-Lake, sure that if there was any place where we could be certain to conceive a child it would be this exquisitely romantic resort.

I think I began to radiate happiness as soon as I arrived, because the love of my life looked my way and asked if I was pleased with the place. How could I not be? The gorgeous views of the lake, the wonderfully attentive staff, the elegance of the decor, and the peacefulness of the setting … it was all so magical. I knew this was going to be the place where our family was to begin.

The suite where we stayed was breathtaking, so spacious and with the finest of furnishings. I already felt like a princess in a fairy tale, and I began to fall in love all over again as my handsome prince carried me across the threshold like a new bride.

And handsome he was. I had to stop and marvel at the man before my eyes. His hair glistened like golden wheat, his eyes as blue as the ocean, and with a warm smile that melted my heart. Yes, indeed, he was a good-looking man, and I, a lucky lady.

Our days were spent like we owned the place, for we did not notice the other guests at the hotel, and our nights were filled with bliss. The only thing that could make it more perfect would be a child that represented our love. My room, this hotel, became my little piece of heaven, and I intended to cherish the whole experience.

It was time for dinner and I wanted to start the evening with a warm bath. I so enjoyed my baths. I had been in the tub for a long time, and when I got out I found my husband had left a note to meet him at the lounge when I was ready. I put on the prettiest dress I had with me, did my hair in an upsweep, and added a little glitter of jewels. I stood back and stared at myself in the mirror. Yes, my husband would be pleased. I did look beautiful, if I might say.

But my buoyant mood was fleeting, because when I entered the lounge I saw my husband with another woman! I didn't want to assume the worst, but the caress of hand against hand, the whispered conversation, and the gentle brush of a kiss upon her cheek as she left suggested intimacy. I couldn't believe what I had just witnessed. Was she the reason he had left me back at the room? Did my husband have feelings for this woman? And who was she? My enchanted evening had just taken a horrible turn, and my stomach knotted in anxiousness.

Trying to act as if I hadn't seen a thing, I casually approached my husband. He smiled, but it had no meaning for this night. The food at dinner was as perfectly prepared as ever, but I tasted nothing but bitter disappointment. My husband tried so hard to make me smile, but all I could think of was the woman that he had brushed up against. We were to go dancing following dinner but I made the excuse that I was not feeling well. He understood, and, tenderly wrapping me in his arms, he guided me back to our room. At one point he gently caressed my face and told me if our child was half as beautiful as I then he would be the luckiest man alive.

I couldn't take it anymore. I demanded to know who the woman was that I had seen him with. He dismissed my question, assuring me it was nothing to worry about. But I did worry, and again I insisted on knowing who the woman was and told him I saw their kiss. My husband froze, a look of fear and surprise etched in his face, but he recovered quickly and told me, with a wave of his hand, that she was simply helping him with a project. By this point I could see that my husband, the man I adored, was hiding something from me.

We argued. He stormed off. I cried and hid in the powder room, remaining there until my eyes were swollen red and I no longer had tears to shed. When I finally emerged, exhausted and confused, I discovered my husband had still not returned. Checking around the hotel, I learned he had taken a rowboat out for a moonlit excursion, perhaps seeking answers in the solitude of the open water and in the gentle lapping of the waves.

Shawl wrapped around my shoulders, I wandered down to the beach, but I saw no sign of a canoe upon the lake. I waited for a while, but the chilly air began creeping through my bones and I thought it best to wait for his return inside. I must have fallen asleep, because the next thing I knew the sun was creeping up over the horizon.

There was a light rapping on the door. Sure that it was my husband and anxious to embrace him, to beg his forgiveness for my jealousy, I jumped from the bed and raced to answer the door. But it wasn't my husband standing before me. Instead it was the same woman that I had seen my husband with the night before. In her arms were dozens of roses, my favourite flower. This, it was clear, was the reason my husband had evaded my questions. He was planning a romantic surprise, and his meeting with the woman was completely innocent. Oh, how I felt foolish. I had to find my love to apologize.

But at this moment the hotel manager arrived, grey-faced and solemn. He was very sorry, he explained, but there had been a terrible accident. My husband's boat had washed ashore upturned, and my husband was presumed drowned. I couldn't believe what I was hearing. He couldn't be dead, he simply couldn't. I had to let him know that I was finally with child, that we were at last going to have the family we craved.

I couldn't deal with what was happening, and I knew I couldn't live life without him. How could I look at my child, see my beloved in its eyes or smile, and be reminded of my loss every time for the rest of my years? How could I raise a child alone, knowing that there should have been someone at my side, and would have been if not for my overreaction and suspicion? I couldn't do it; I couldn't live without him. And so my mind was made up. I walked to the water's edge. It was almost as if the lake … or perhaps my husband lying beneath its waves … was calling to me, so I kept walking until the waters took hold of me and never let go.

Today, I still walk the water's edge, still looking for my love to return so we could once again be the family we were meant to be.[5]

Other psychics seem to reinforce elements of this story. Pauline Raby, a noted medium and founder of the Feng Shui and Energy Centre of Canada, corroborated key elements while conducting research alongside paranormal investigator John Savoie for the book *Shadows of Niagara*.[6] Raby believes the woman was named Annabelle or Anna, and that she didn't have the opportunity to say goodbye to a loved one. "There is a tremendous loss … there is grief, separation," she felt. And beyond psychic impression, Pauline also came back from her research with audio proof of a ghostly presence at the gazebo in the form of Electronic Voice Phenomenon (EVP). A tape recording made that night clearly picked up a female voice saying, "Come back, I'm sorry."[7] It seems that Annabelle or Anna, or whatever name the ghostly woman went by in life, is bound to

Bathing Beach, Queens Royal Hotel, Niagara-On-The-Lake, Canada.

The placid image on this turn-of-the-century postcard does nothing to hint at the tragic story that played out on this very beach.

the shoreline and won't leave until her husband returns from the watery depths that swallowed him.

It's possible that this tragic woman isn't the only spirit inhabiting Queen's Royal Park. Some townsfolk have also claimed to hear the calls of soldiers and seen men in uniforms lingering on the grounds late at night. It's uncertain why undead soldiers may want to linger here because, as far as is known, there were no skirmishes here during the War of 1812. Still, folklore persists that the ghosts seen so often late on moonless nights are American troops who died while wading ashore, their feet having yet to touch the land they gave their lives to occupy.[8]

But ghostly soldiers are hardly unique in Niagara-on-the-Lake, which perhaps explains why the story of the painfully tormented spectral woman is by far the most popular paranormal story to be associated with Queen's Royal Park. It may also be because her story — full of drama and passion, tragedy and loss — simply pulls at the heartstrings in powerful ways, dealing with emotions that all of us can relate to. Perhaps it is both.

Few can deny that Queen's Royal Park is a beautiful locale, and that the Lakefront Gazebo provides the perfect vantage point from which to

The Queen's Royal Hotel was once one of Canada's finest resorts, a place of elegance, romance, and, on occasion, tragedy.

enjoy the view. People have appreciated the undeniably romantic appeal of the area seemingly forever. In the early years, well-to-do couples staying at the Queen's Royal Hotel would stroll arm-in-arm along the beach in a courtship that was impeccably mannered and yet still intimate. Today, the gazebo plays host to youthful dates where love is tentatively explored and to countless memorable weddings where love is affirmed before friends and family.

But that is during the day. At night, when shadows stretch across the landscape, the romance gives way to sadness and even fear. Young lovers sitting along the water's edge may find their solitude suddenly interrupted by a woman walking along the shoreline. The intrusion is bad enough, but worse is the realization that they can see straight through her to the lapping waves beyond. She fixes a cold stare, a terrifying stare, at the young couple. No harm is intended, but she longs for love she lost so long ago and watching demonstrations of affection adds to her suffering. Panicked, all thoughts of intimacy now vanished, the teenage lovers bolt from the beach. The ghost is left alone on the beach once again, and alone she will remain for all eternity.

6
PRINCE OF WALES HOTEL

The woman is stunningly beautiful, but her angelic features are shadowed by great sadness. She wanders the Prince of Wales Hotel almost aimlessly, oblivious to those around her and to the luxurious surroundings. Guests can't help but notice her tears, and wonder why she could be so upset while in such a beautiful place. She walks back and forth through the hallways, as if desperately seeking something, or someone. Hearts go out to her, and guests want to console her. But as they reach out to lay a gentle hand upon her slender shoulder, she suddenly fades from view. Who is this woman, and what is her connection to the Prince of Wales?

They say love conquers all, but can it survive death? Staff and guests of the elegant hotel have no doubt that it most certainly can, and look to this devoted woman as proof. Her love is so intense that it survived not only her beloved's death but even her own, and keeps her bound to the enchanting location where they spent their final tearful moments. The mournful ghost glides through the hotel's richly wooded hallways, her mind reliving cherished moments with her beloved, awaiting the return of a husband decades overdue. She refuses to give up her vigil, convinced they will be together again if only she remains patient and waits a little while longer. But it's never to be. Instead, the woman's tireless devotion and obvious suffering tug at the heartstrings of all those who encounter her, her sadness so out of place in what must surely be one of the loveliest hotels imaginable.

Her story doesn't begin with sadness, however.[1] Just the opposite, it begins with the euphoria that only love can bring. It was during the dark days of the First World War that a young local woman fell passionately and deeply in love with a soldier training at nearby Camp Niagara for overseas duty.[2] Pretty and charming, she could have had any man she wanted, but she chose him. What had started as a friendship quickly turned into something more intimate. They were young and their hearts were filled with love; days were spent in euphoric bliss, and evenings were filled by dreams for their future.

But a dark cloud hovered over their courtship, for the woman knew that her beloved would soon be pulled from her arms to fight in a war that seemed, to her young mind, senseless and so very far away. She chose not to focus on their eventual parting and instead attempted to cherish the short time they had together. As the day of his departure grew near, the lovers made a quick decision: they would marry, so that when he was overseas they would be together in matrimony, if not in person.

They had long planned how they would make their union special, but such fanciful dreams had to be put aside because the young groom was only on a short leave before he would be sent overseas. The Prince of Wales was selected as both the venue for the ceremony and the honeymoon destination; circumstances dictated that the soldier could not provide his bride with the kind of wedding all young girls dream of while growing up, but he was determined she would have some luxury on her special day. With only her family in attendance, they held hands (she not wanting to ever let go) and, with only a few spoken words in a hasty ceremony, became husband and wife.

There were only a few stolen moments in between the young groom's formal duties, but his bride made the best out of the minutes they shared. The tender encounters only made her heart ache more, because she knew he would soon leave the comforts of her arms and take up arms in the name of their country. The night before he was to board a train for Halifax — to be transported by ship to the killing fields of France — the soldier said a tearful farewell to his new bride. He swore he would return to her after the war's end, and she vowed to remain true to him until such day as they were together once more. She would wait till eternity, if need be, she swore.

Even as the months of waiting turned into a year, the young woman remained desperately in love. She wrote letters daily, and spent much of her free time imagining the happy reunion. Not for a moment did she entertain the possibility that her husband may not return; she was convinced their love would see him through any danger.

But then a cable arrived, which brought her the sad news that the soldier had been killed amongst the barbed wire and mud-filled trenches of Europe. She refused to believe it. He had promised to return to her arms. He had promised. He had never gone back on his word before and the woman knew in her heart that he wouldn't do so now. And so she waited for his arrival, convinced the cable had been an error. Most of her time was spent in her room in the hotel, alone with her cherished memories and with letters so stained by tears that the ink upon them had begun to run. The locals of Niagara-on-the-Lake became accustomed to her sad, expectant face staring out at tree-lined Picton Street between slightly parted curtains. Guests in the hotel frequently heard sorrowful sobs late at night as she cried herself to sleep.

As hope for her husband's return dwindled, the woman grew thinner and quieter, withdrawing almost completely into an inner world where she relived passionate moments from their too-brief time together. Soon she couldn't bear to leave her room, and in time she died in there, a photo of her husband clutched firmly to her chest. She had perished believing to the end that her husband was still alive and had neglected to fulfill his promise to her. Her reluctance to give up her wait prevented her spirit from leaving the hotel and she remains bound there still.

At least there is some comfort. The woman is hardly alone, as thousands of tourists come to Niagara-on-the-Lake every year to experience the timeless hospitality and enduring charm of the Prince of Wales Hotel. Some actually envy the ghost; reluctant to leave the enchanting resort, they wish they, too, could remain lifelong guests.

The Prince of Wales is the most elegant of Niagara's hotels and has long been a cherished historical landmark to both residents of Niagara-on-the-Lake and travellers from around the world. Its reputation for hospitality is unparalleled, its splendour breathtaking. And yet it had humble beginnings in 1864 as Long's Hotel, a common inn frequented by common folk.[3]

Over the next few decades, the fortunes of Niagara-on-the-Lake changed dramatically as it evolved into a popular tourist destination in the latter half

Originally built as Long's Hotel in the nineteenth century, the Prince of Wales Hotel is a landmark in Niagara-on-the-Lake. The cornerstone with the date of construction inscribed on it can still be seen today.

of the nineteenth century. People from as far away as the southern United States and Europe arrived in droves every year to enjoy the relatively warm climate, bask in the beauty of the town and its surroundings, and make the short trip to take in the breathtaking splendour of the nearby falls. Accustomed to the finer things in life, these wealthy vacationers demanded luxury accommodations, fine dining, and activities in keeping with their stature. It was during this era of prosperity that Long's Hotel was transformed into an elegant property catering to the well-to-do.[4]

Undoubtedly the wealthiest and most important guest during this era of extravagance was the Prince of Wales, the future King George V and the son of Queen Victoria, who enjoyed an extensive stay at the hotel in 1901 with his wife, Queen Mary. To commemorate this event, around 1920 the owners elected to change the hotel's name in honour of the Royals.[5] It seemed only fitting — a regal name for a majestic hotel.

But hard as it is to believe today, the establishment fell on hard times in the 1920s as many of the wealthy patrons found other ways to spend their vacation. This was followed by the Great Depression, which reduced its owners to the verge of bankruptcy. The hotel actually remained closed for the

1934 season, such was the desperate state of affairs, and the future seemed anything but bright.

Thankfully, the succession of owners that followed always found a way to keep the grand old hotel open, even if with each passing year it was further and further removed from its heyday of the Victorian era. In 1975, the Wiens family purchased the Prince of Wales, and it remained in their hands for twenty-two years. They put their heart and soul, as well as considerable amounts of money, into saving the aging structure, which by then was a mere shadow of its former self. They had a vision of returning the Prince of Wales to the important monument it once was, and to that end they not only refurbished the building, but also expanded it down King Street in one direction and down Picton in the other to include what we now know as the South Wing, the Studio, and the Court buildings.[6]

In March of 1997, it was added to the Vintage Hotel properties, joining the Queen's Landing and Pillar and Post to create a new standard of elegance and sophistication in the Niagara Region. On November 8, 1998, the doors of the Prince of Wales were closed in order to complete an extensive restoration project designed to transform it into a building that captures the true essence of Victorian charm. When the doors swung open once again on July 1, 1999, visitors stepped into beauty beyond one's imagination, a truly enchanting hotel where one can actually believe — if only for the duration of their stay — that dreams really can come true.[7]

Sadly, the resident ghost's dream of being reunited with her loved one is one that cannot be fulfilled, and her melancholy prevents her from enjoying the charm of her surroundings. Her stay is not one of relaxation and pleasure, but rather an enduring torment from which there seems to be no escape.[8]

The spectral woman is felt most often in the elegant main lobby, and at least on one occasion guests have been greeted upon their arrival by the sight of a beautiful, young, ethereal woman wearing an outdated floor-length dress wandering the lobby. She is also said to linger upstairs in Room 207, and has also been seen sitting comfortably in the bar, oblivious to the world around her. Some guests have even seen her ghostly image peering out a window onto the street, as if still expecting to see her loved one returning to her after all these years.

It's said that as late as 2002, there were still patrons checking out at 2:00 a.m. due to ghostly inconveniences, but no one we spoke to had heard of anything so drastic.

"This did not happen to me, but to my aunt and uncle who stayed at the Prince of Wales," says a young woman who sent us an email in response to our call for Niagara-on-the-Lake ghost experiences. "So, it all started when my aunt and uncle were sleeping at night. The bed would shake, like when someone tries to wake you up. My aunt woke up and thought it was my uncle, but he was sound asleep. It happened a few times. The last time, my aunt felt cold hands under the blankets and saw the face of a woman leaning over the bed. No body, just a face. It scared my aunt and she couldn't sleep again that night."

Could this have been the ghost that many have sensed in the hotel? And was she possibly upset by the presence of a couple in her domain, enjoying each other's company? She longs to feel the arms of her husband wrapped around her once more, so perhaps companionship in any form, even something as simple as man and woman sleeping contently side-by-side, causes her pain and anguish.

Reports of sightings of the spectral woman are rare, but her antics are not. She tends to make her presence known at night in various ways: following staff around, moving objects, and even rapping on patron's doors. For a former staff member, a skeptic at first, a single inexplicable event was enough to make her a believer in the paranormal. She was at the front desk when she heard her name being called out by a woman's voice. The voice sounded as if it had come from behind her, but when the clerk turned around no one was there. It was in the evening, the lobby was quiet, and there were no guests or staff around. How does one explain that rationally? This woman couldn't. Nor could she explain the sudden unease she felt, as if she were being watched. In that instant, she knew ghosts truly existed and that the Prince of Wales lives up to his haunted reputation.

Today, Shane Howard is the front office manager at the Pillar and Post, a sister hotel in the Vintage Hotel family, but he was formerly employed at the Prince of Wales, and it was here, in the winter of 1999, that he had an experience that left him bewildered and not a little shaken. Even years later, Shane struggles to make sense of that evening's events.

"I was working three to eleven p.m. and Ms. Lai, the owner, was in the dining room with her guests. Later into the evening she asked me to show them a guest room, so I went up to Room 207 (the room with a balcony overlooking the road) to turn the lights on and ensure it looked perfect," he recalls, thinking back to that night. "When I came down from the room in the elevator, Ms. Lai and her guests were there waiting for me to take them up to the room. It was no more than three minutes later. We entered the suite and went into the bedroom. The lamp next to the bed was turned off (the light bulb didn't burn out, as I turned the light back on and it worked fine) and the chair from the desk by the bed had been moved over about four feet nearer to the bed. Since I was just in the room minutes prior, I would have noticed both of these things. Ms. Lai and I both looked at each other and thought this was a little spooky."

Shane knew that he had left the room in ideal condition and that no member of the staff would pull such a prank, especially when those being shown the room were guests of the owner and wealthy business people representing potential clients. Shane also knew that the room was well known for its haunted activity and that people entering the room become aware of a strong presence said to be the ghost of a lonesome woman. He's convinced that the mischievous individual who put the room in disarray was otherworldly in origin, perhaps letting the Prince of Wales staff know that Room 207 is hers until she chooses to check out.

Our final story involves a woman who spent a couple of autumn nights at the Prince of Wales. Julia arrived on a chilly day, the kind where you tug the zipper of your jacket up close to your neck, but as soon as she entered the hotel, the goose bumps covering her skin were melted by overwhelming warmth. It wasn't so much the temperature that made her suddenly feel toasty, but rather the inviting atmosphere of the hotel and the excitement over being in such an enchanting building.

She was instantly struck by the elegance of the lobby: beautiful stained glass windows, a flawless bronze statue depicting a small child sitting as she reads the book in her hands, and a white marble statue of two young lovers passionately embracing. What a wonderful area, she thought, while taking

To enter the Prince of Wales is to experience the timeless hospitality of the Victorian era. Warm and refined, it's little wonder that at least one guest has refused to check out even after death.

it all in. Just being there made Julia feel like a princess in a castle, but like any castle, the Prince of Wales has its share of mysteries hidden within, and it wasn't long before she accidentally uncovered one.

Julia spent some time exploring the magnificent historical building, and found her breath taken away by its many lavish details. Suddenly, she came upon an area where she just didn't feel the same. Her previous excitement started to slowly drain away as another feeling settled in. It was an uncomfortable and overwhelming sense of something lost; something that, despite years of searching, could not be found. The feelings were strongest in the lobby, which only minutes before had felt so soothing and inviting. Julia could feel someone's pain and sorrow over the absence of someone deeply loved, and regret at not having had the opportunity to explore that love through a lifetime together. She got the impression — and could have sworn she saw the faint, wispy outline — of a love-sick soul lingering in the lobby awaiting someone's return.

The feeling didn't last long, it came and went in a matter of minutes, but Julia was sure of what she felt, and it left her on the verge of tears. She imagined a woman waiting patiently by the doors, perhaps sitting in one of the more comfortable chairs, watching all the guests come and go, hoping one of them might be her love.

This unfortunate ghost remains behind on the earthly plane, still believing that one day the promise her husband made to return to her might be fulfilled. Ironically, the only thing keeping the lovers apart is her devotion that endures so strongly even after decades of separation. If the ghostly woman would only let go of it, her spirit would pass from the realm of the living and be reunited with her beloved on the other side, where he no doubt waits for her as faithfully as she does him.

7
FORT MISSISSAUGA

Autumn was a forgotten dream as a cutting wind off Lake Ontario howled through the ruined fortress and cut through jackets and sweaters. The sky overhead was grey and ominous, and constant flurries danced across the early November landscape. The brisk cold hurried the pace of the two tourists — a man and woman — intent on experiencing Fort Mississauga, but even the short walk left their toes and fingers numb.

The man became engrossed in reading the plaques describing the history and importance of the fort, and his discomfort was soon forgotten. The woman became distracted as well. She instinctively knew they were not alone in the fort, and scanned the area for another person foolish enough to brave the cold. There was no one to be seen; the fort was empty except for herself and her friend, and the only footprints in the fresh snow were theirs. She began to shiver. Not from the cold, but rather from a grave-like chill that arose from within her being. Perhaps it was the wind, but she felt as though an icy hand touched her spine. Something terrible has happened here, she thought to herself; someone died painfully.

The act of grabbing her friend's hand was a silent request to leave. But as they walked away she risked one last look over her shoulder. Her face went white, so ghostly pale that it looked like a mask of snow, while her eyes widened in disbelief because, through the flurries, she saw a young man looking down at them from atop the earthen parapet that surrounds the fort. He was bare-chested despite the frosty temperature, and his trousers were blood-soaked. The woman shuddered in horror. Panic threatened to take hold of her senses. Gripping her friend's hand tighter, she urged him to pick up the pace. She wanted nothing more than to flee from the fort's aging stones and oppressive walls. The memories of that chilling day remain with her still.

There are certain structures that convey a ghostly presence. Fort Mississauga is one such place. On dreary, grey days or under the pale light of the moon, the ancient fortress takes on a surprisingly sinister appearance. It feels cold and menacing somehow, as if it resents the intrusion into its brooding. And there is a strong presence of something not quite human; you feel it as soon as you step through the yawning gates, and the eerie sensation remains with you through the duration of your exploration of the fort.

Fort Mississauga is a national historic site, but unlike many fortresses of its era — Fort York in Toronto, Fort Henry in Kingston, and nearby Fort George — it hasn't been restored nor is it a well-known tourist attraction. In fact, it lies almost forgotten and in a state of disrepair amidst the grounds of the Niagara-on-the-Lake Golf Club, a rarely visited relic of yesteryear.[1] A pathway leads from the corner of Simcoe and Front Streets, through a fairway, to the shores of Lake Ontario and the fort's imposing walls. While most of the buildings have long since rotted away, visitors are free to explore the earthworks, enter tunnels (one of which emerges onto the lakeshore), marvel at the imposing concrete tower, and tour a powder magazine.[2] Pretty soon, one begins to gain an appreciation for the history that lies within these eerie ruins ... and for the darkness that envelops them.

Fort Mississauga was built during the War of 1812 and was designed to improve British defences along the Niagara Frontier. In particular, it was intended to become a replacement for Fort George, which had proven to be highly vulnerable. During the American invasion, much of it had been destroyed. The impressive artillery-proof central tower, the centrepiece of Fort Mississauga, took shape in 1814 using as its foundation fire-blackened bricks and stones salvaged from the ruins of Niagara-on-the-Lake, burned to the ground the year before by American forces, and from a lighthouse that once stood on the site.[3] Fort Mississauga was born of tragedy, and from the very beginning its cold stone walls were stained with death and despair.

When completed just after the war ended in early 1815, Fort Mississauga served as a vital strongpoint in a defence system that extended along the Great Lakes. A British garrison was maintained at Fort Mississauga almost constantly until 1855, at which point it was taken over by Canadian militia units.[4] During the twentieth century, by which time its earthworks and stone walls had become obsolete and the enemy it was built to defend against was no longer a threat, Fort Mississauga was used as a training facility by the Canadian military. Thousands of young men passed through here on their way to distant battlefields during both World Wars and the Korean War. Many never returned. But despite having never been besieged by an enemy army or bombarded by artillery,[5] Fort Mississauga has seen its share of misery and death. This tragic history is fertile ground for ghost stories.

One terrifying story supposedly dates back to 1814, at which time the War of 1812 was still raging.[6] During that year, a young British soldier, little more than a boy really, suddenly found himself pulled from the loving arms of his mother and taken from his home in the hills of northern England by the British Army. Though not yet old enough to shave, he was deemed old enough to carry a musket and so was sent to the bloodstained battlefields of Niagara-on-the-Lake. During his first taste of battle, the young soldier watched in horror as his comrades fought and died all around him. The noise was terrifying — the crackling roar of musket fire, the screams of wounded men, officers yelling orders. A filthy bank of rolling smoke coughed out by hundreds of musket muzzles obscured his vision, adding to the terror. The boy knew what he had to do, what his duty required him to do, but his thoughts kept going back to his mother and her final words, "Please come home safely." He wanted so much for this nightmare to be over, to once again be in the safety of his home. Courage failed him, and rather than stand and face the enemy fire, he took cover from the hail of bullets, ensuring his survival but turning his back on his comrades and his duty as a soldier. He knew it was cowardice, but he didn't care.

The regiment's superior officer had noticed the young soldier's failure to perform his duty and decided to make an example of him. Cowardice would not be permitted, not in his regiment. The officer ordered the young soldier taken back to Fort Mississauga and there had the entire regiment assembled to observe him being viciously flogged. The soldiers watching the brutal punishment were silent and sullen. They felt the punishment harsh and unjust, and they hated the officer for ordering it. But the officer didn't care. He believed that power did not lie in being liked, but in being feared, and he was determined to instill discipline and honour among his soldiers.

Screams pierced the silence as the lashes landed on bare flesh, one after the other. The young soldier stared with loathing at the commanding officer and his subordinates, but none of them looked at him. They tried to ignore the sight of a man, a boy, being beaten in front of them. Each blow of the leather sliced into the mess of broken flesh and ribboned skin, and more gleaming blood spurted away. When he was finally cut down after countless lashes, his back had been transformed into a maze of bloody wounds. The boy's limp body collapsed into the blood that had dripped from his injuries and pooled at his feet. He drew his last breath as his grim-faced comrades walked away with heavy hearts. They couldn't help but feel pity for the boy who would never return home to England or to the loving arms of his mother.

Neither did his soul. It remains tied to Fort Mississauga, doomed forever to wander the grounds — a ghostly soldier defending the place from a non-existent enemy. The trauma of his death seems to be mirrored in the frightening experiences of those who encounter him. On some evenings the soldier's pain-filled cries echo across the centuries, occasionally accompanied by the sound of an invisible whip cracking. On other nights, when a storm is raging, or a deathly chill hangs in the air, his pitiful apparition appears on the earthworks at Fort Mississauga, clothes bloodstained and hanging in ribbons from his flayed back.

One of the earliest documented sightings of a ghostly soldier at Fort Mississauga dates back to June 11, 1871, when Private Andrew Greenhill and another soldier were ordered to stand guard at the fort.

"The first two hours off, Jim and I spread our blankets together on the hard oak floor and slept as sound as a top the whole time," he wrote in a journal entry reprinted in *Canadian Military History*. "We had to turn out at 2:00 a.m. Jim was put on the gate and I on the ramparts. It was pitch dark and the time dragged wearily along. The only sound that broke the deathlike stillness was the waves washing against the lakefront of the fort. The only things we saw in that long two hours were a dog and a tall figure in a black robe. It glided along the top of the wall swiftly and was seen by Jim as well as myself. My knees shook under me. I fixed my bayonet, gave chase and challenged it, but it glided out of sight and left me more frightened than ever. We said nothing to the guard about it after, being afraid of ridicule."[7]

That fear of ridicule has no doubt kept many people from coming forward over the years with their own experiences with the ghostly residents of Fort Mississauga. One person who overcame this natural hesitancy shared with us an unusual story.

October is a transitional month. The air this time of year is cool and crisp, neither hot nor cold, the bright colours of the fall leaves are slowly fading as trees become barren and skeletal. The month brings beauty, but it also reminds us that the bitter cold winter months are just around the corner — a time when nature culls the weak and the sick.

It's believed that during the October witching season the veil separating the realms of the living and the dead becomes thinner, and that spirits straddle these two worlds and are more active as a consequence. Perhaps unsurprising, an unusual number of experiences have occurred at Fort Mississauga over the years.

In early October 2014, when the leaves had turned a painter's palette of colours and the summer hordes had disappeared from the streets of Niagara-on-the-Lake, paranormal investigator Ian Russell wandered through the remains of the eerily silent fort, audio recorder in hand. He ventured in the dark depths of the powder magazine and there, enveloped by shadows, he recorded one of the best EVPs he'd ever heard. A voice, distinctly British, came from out of the gloom: "Who's there?" Unlike with so many EVP recordings, the words are not open to interpretation, but clear and intelligible. Even years later, the paranormal investigator admits that merely thinking about the encounter gives him chills.

A few years later, in late October, another paranormal investigator decided to venture out to Fort Mississauga. Nick and his companion, a woman who asked to remain anonymous, were eager to have an experience, but at the same time didn't expect too much, as they had conducted numerous investigations over the years and came away disappointed with nothing more than a few anomalies on their equipment — nothing dramatic or exciting enough to be worth talking about it.

It was late, approximately 12:40 a.m. The cool night air caused their breaths to cloud before their faces. Guided by the beam of their flashlights, Nick took the lead in making their way to Fort Mississauga and straight toward the powder room to see what kind of paranormal activity they could discover.

Nick felt a sense of history within the two-hundred-year-old room and felt his mind going back to the War of 1812. He imagined a thunderous roar as cannons boomed and the panic soldiers would have felt as cannonballs from the opposite shore barrelled toward them. He was pulled from his thoughts when his friend spoke his name.

Nick turned to look at his friend to answer her and almost jumped out of his skin when he saw a shadow glide across the wall in the depths of the magazine. The shadow was very pronounced and distinctly human shaped. Nick almost jumped in fright. He spun around quickly to see who was behind him to cast the shadow, but no one was there. Could this be the very thing these two companions had waited so long for? After a few long seconds of fear and confusion, Nick finally found the words that were trapped in his throat to ask his friend, "Did you see that?"

The woman had a very perplexed expression on her face. "See what?" she whispered back. She hadn't seen the shadow slide along the wall and didn't understand why Nick had spun around so suddenly or what he was referring to.

At that moment Nick realized something. Since the only light came from the flashlights that they were holding, there was no way anyone could cast a shadow unless they were standing between them and the wall! The size of the shadow Nick had seen fleetingly appeared to indicate that it belonged to someone — or something — tall in stature. For someone to come into the powder magazine and go undetected was next to impossible; the chamber is small and even for two individuals it was quite cramped. A third person couldn't step inside and not be noticed.

Nick's arms were covered in goose bumps, as if the temperature had suddenly plummeted, and a strong gust of wind pushed back the hood of his coat. Except there was no wind that night. It was eerily still. And, of course, they were sheltered within the powder magazine.

Nick had been anxious to experience the paranormal, but now it wasn't quite the thrill he thought it would be. He was terrified. Nick decided they'd had enough for one evening. "This doesn't feel right," he said, with a mouth suddenly gone dry. "It's time to leave."

When the two companions stepped out of the magazine, they noticed that a light dusting of snow had fallen. The pale moon from above and the beams of their flashlights reflected off the snow, helping to chase away some of the darkness. Nick found the brightness of the crisp, clean, white snow refreshing, and as they made their way back to the car, he found that the fear that had gripped him was slowly beginning to subside.

Then, suddenly, he stopped in his tracks. He grabbed his partner by her shoulders and turned her toward him. "Did you hear that?" he whispered earnestly, fear once again threatening to overwhelm him. Nick found some comfort in the fearful look on his friend's face, knowing that this time he wasn't alone and that she, too, had heard it: the sound of crunching snow, like someone was walking behind them, trailing them, maybe even stalking them.

They turned slowly and, with their flashlights, began to scan over the area. In the dusting of freshly fallen snow they spotted a set of tracks in their wake, as if someone had been following them. At first, they thought perhaps the footprints could have been made by someone earlier that evening and had simply been revealed by the blowing wind, but when they looked closer the startled pair realized this was unlikely — the tracks seemed to have stopped midstride, as if the person suddenly disappeared.

Could this have been made by the shadow that Nick had spotted fleetingly in the magazine? If so, was the shade following them, perhaps even stalking them, from the darkness? To what end? Nick and his companion couldn't know for sure, but they knew that on this day in late October they had found the one thing they had longed for: a spine-chilling paranormal experience.

It was in July 2007 when Stan Kuziw took his wife and son to explore Fort Mississauga. Even though it was a beautiful summer day, Stan felt uneasy. "I got the strange sensation someone was at my side, walking beside me on my right," he remembers. "It was enough to get my hair rising and I decided I had to come back that night." With the disappearance of the sun's comforting light, Stan's wife and son refused to leave the car, leaving

The evocative remains of Fort Mississauga, where a flogged soldier and a headless First Nations warrior appear on storm-tossed nights.

Stan to explore on his own. It wasn't long before he began to question the wisdom of going alone. "I was along the path leading to the fort when I got the strangest feeling. You know that musty smell you get in an old house? That's what it smelled like," he explains. "I was taking random pictures and got lots of orbs in the middle of the path, as well as a few images with pairs of red eyes looking at me, and in another the shape of what looks like people walking toward me."

Suddenly, when he was about a hundred feet from the fort's front gates, his cameras went dead. Not just one, which would have been inconvenient but not exactly unusual, but three cameras — at the exact same time. Stan continued on and then saw ... something. "It came up and went over the gate, flying up toward the right. I thought at first it was a bird, trying to be rational, you know. But I knew it wasn't a bird because it didn't have wings. What it really looked like was an all-black torso." Stan didn't linger long, and began the walk back to the car and his awaiting family. While leaving, he was surprised to find his cameras working again, so he decided to quickly return and take a few final photos of the gloomy fort. At the exact same spot where it had happened just minutes before, the camera batteries died again. That was it for Stan. He felt unwelcome and left for good. "That place is definitely very busy," he says. "The spirits there just don't want people around. It felt as if they were telling me to leave."[8]

That's a feeling many get at Fort Mississauga: a sense that they are intruding on sacred, sanctified ground and that the souls tied to it prefer not to have their seclusion intruded upon. It's certainly a feeling Nicole (who asked that her real name not be used) is familiar with, having explored the fort numerous times during her childhood, growing up in Niagara-on-the-Lake. On one occasion, she ignored the foreboding sensation, and the results were chilling, to say the least.

It was a chilly winter dawn when Nicole began her walk through the snow-frosted grounds of Niagara-on-the-Lake Golf Club. As a child, she always enjoyed the dungeon-like tunnels below Fort Mississauga, so she decided to relive her childhood memories and delve into them. It was a decision that would bring her face to face with the fort's tragic past.

Ducking her head, she disappeared into the dark tunnel leading to the fort's powder magazine. Ice clung to the aging stone, and the temperature dropped noticeably, even though she was out of the numbing wind. She emerged into the small chamber at the end of the corridor, noting that it hadn't changed in the years since her childhood. As she turned to leave, she saw a dark, menacing silhouette standing at the tunnel entrance. Terror gripped Nicole as the figure floated toward her. The closer it got, the more clearly she could make out features — a tattered red uniform, dull eyes, face shadowed by anger. The ghost reached out to Nicole. She retreated, but when her back pressed against cold stone walls, she realized she had nowhere left to go. The apparition continued to advance. Its hand was now inches from Nicole's face. A raspy whisper escaped from its lifeless throat. Then, just as she expected to feel the grip of cold, bony hands on her throat, the ghost faded into nothingness.[9]

Another legend suggests that there is a particular spot where, if you were to stand upon it after the sun had set, you would hear battle being raged. Sometimes this location is identified within the earthen walls of the fort, other times on the surrounding golf course. Here, the sounds of musket fire,

Emerging into the light from a tunnel leading to the powder vault. The eerie tunnel, dark and chilled even on the brightest day, has been the scene of countless frightening encounters with otherworldly presences.

the thunder-like rumble of cannons, officers' shouted orders, and the screams of the wounded fill the night air. The turmoil is too close to be that of some far-off re-enactment; instead, it feels as though one is in the very heart of a life-or-death struggle being fought by invisible armies, as if fighting and dying is taking place all around you, unseen but within reach. There's historical precedent for this. On May 27, 1813, an American force under Brigadier General George McClure came ashore here, and heavy fighting took place upon the very grounds that are today encompassed by Fort Mississauga and the golf course.

The final documented spirit is that of a headless First Nations warrior, whose tormented soul remains bound to the spot of his horrific death. Even before the War of 1812 erupted, the British Indian Department worked hard to secure the allegiance of the various First Nations. They realized that, in the event of hostilities with America, the assistance of their warriors, battle hardened and brave, would be a vital source of manpower to supplement their meagre force of regulars and militia.

The Six Nations of the Grand River, under Chief John Norton, were among the first to come to British aid after the United States declared war.[10] They were intimately connected with events along the Niagara River, since their forebears had crossed the river as refugees from the American government in 1784 to make new homes under British protection. As early as July, one hundred Grand River warriors made camp here on the grounds of what later became Fort Mississauga. By autumn this number had swelled to four hundred.

When the Battle of Queenston Heights began on October 13, Norton, along with about eighty warriors, raced to the scene of the fighting. The others milled about their encampment in Niagara-on-the-Lake, unsure of what to do, uncommitted to the battle. They could hear the distant fight, the muskets snapping and shells exploding dully to the south. Did they want to die for the British, who had not always been the most faithful of allies? Most were not yet decided.

Suddenly, there came the deafening ripple of cannon fire from across the river and the opposite shore became fogged by a white cloud of smoke. American artillery was firing upon Fort George and the village of Niagara-on-the-Lake. The noise was deafening as round shot screamed across the river and crashed into buildings, splintered trees, and crumbled brickwork. British cannons responded in kind.

The First Nations people watched the artillery duel, mesmerized by its ferocity and destructive power. No fire was directed at their encampment, so they seemed apart from the fighting. That changed in an instant when an American ball fell short of Niagara-on-the-Lake and found a human target instead as it whipped through the crowd of milling onlookers. A red mist appeared in the air as the ball took a man's head clean off. He staggered for a second, then finally collapsed. The cannonball lay embedded in the soil a short distance away, smeared with blood.[11] A ghost was born. Since then, the pitiful headless spirit has been seen numerous times, walking aimlessly around the ruins of the old fort.

When night settles upon Fort Mississauga, it seems to awaken something. The atmosphere changes, becoming oppressive and unnatural, and shadowy figures are fleetingly seen amidst the gloom. Though the fort was never put to the test in battle, the land upon which it stands, and even the stones with which it was built, have felt the Reaper's touch of death: soldiers who fell in battle, a young life cut short by cruel punishment, civilians displaced by war, and a headless warrior. Is it any wonder then that Fort Mississauga is one of Niagara-on-the-Lake's most chilling locales?

8
NIAGARA APOTHECARY

The handsome gentleman wearing a dark suit and holding a cane in one hand stood in the corner of the historic apothecary on a spring afternoon in 1998, the museum filled with tourists. He was a pleasant-looking man who would occasionally smile at other folk, but kept to himself and never said a word. The gentleman seemed to be completely engrossed in the various displays depicting a nineteenth-century drugstore.

A family visiting Niagara-on-the-Lake at the time found themselves taken with the unique history of the Niagara Apothecary, so they began taking numerous photos of the interior. The distinguished gentleman found himself in several frames — he seemed so immersed in his own little world that the family couldn't bring themselves to ask him to step aside.

Strangely enough, when the photos were developed sometime later, the cane-carrying man was nowhere to be seen! Everyone in the family had expected him to be in three or four photos, and yet he wasn't even in one. The only evidence — startling as it was — that he had ever really been there was found in a single image where a vague, misty shape occupied the very spot where the gentleman had stood. The family debated the matter for a while, wondering if perhaps there was a logical explanation. In the end they realized that the proof was in the pictures: they had seen, and partially photographed, an apparition![1]

The Niagara Apothecary re-creates a nineteenth-century pharmacy. Ghostly footsteps, flitting shadows, and the inexplicable scent of belladonna suggest the living history museum comes complete with a resident of the past.

Unbeknownst to this family, others have experienced the presence of the Niagara Apothecary ghost. These people have come to realize that not all history and ghosts in Niagara-on-the-Lake are connected to the War of 1812. Instead, they can be found in the charming homes and shops that line the streets — among them the Niagara Apothecary.

The apothecary is one of Canada's oldest continuously serving drugstores, and certainly the oldest in Ontario. Until 1865, the building had served as a customs building and the office of Judge Edward Campbell, but it was purchased that year by Henry Paffard and remodelled to serve as a new home for his thriving drugstore. Paffard, and the five pharmacists who followed in his footsteps, served Niagara-on-the-Lake by dispensing pills and providing medicines to the ill. It was a profitable trade, and an important one for the health and well-being of the community.

After nearly a hundred years in operation, the pharmacy finally closed in 1964. Recognizing its historic value, the Ontario College of Pharmacists purchased the building and, with the assistance of the Ontario Heritage Foundation, restored the building and reopened it as a museum in 1971.[2] Almost all of the fixtures, black walnut countertop, and store clock are original and date back to 1865. In addition, many early account ledgers and prescription books, as well as an impressive collection of jars and bottles from the old business, have been recovered and are now on display. The result is a museum that transports visitors back in time to an authentic nineteenth-century apothecary so that even though it no longer carries on its former trade, the building looks as it did a century ago. As a result, the apothecary belongs to the past as much as to the present, and as much to the spirits of yesterday as to the tourists of today.

Staff members and visitors alike have noted strange events there ever since it opened as a museum. Oftentimes, early in the morning or after closing in the evening, the distinct sound of footsteps is heard treading overhead. Since they should be alone in the building at these hours, these sounds alarm the on-duty staff members, but upon investigation they find their fear is unfounded as there is never anyone to be found on the second floor.

Footsteps are also frequently heard on the staircase leading to the second floor. Generally it is just the measured pace of someone casually walking, but sometimes it is the heavy and hasty tread of someone running. Once, staff members even decided to test for the presence of ghosts by carefully placing newspapers over the steps. When they returned the following morning, the pages had been disturbed by unseen footsteps ... proof, at least, that they weren't losing their minds by imagining the inexplicable sounds.

But noises aren't the only unusual phenomena that unsettles staff members and visitors. Icy-cold spots in an otherwise warm building are a frequent complaint, and there have been reports of unusual flashes of light near the back of the building. And then there is the smell of belladonna that many people notice. Otherwise known as deadly nightshade, this herb is no longer kept on the premises — despite being an authentic nineteenth-century curative — because of the danger it poses if ingested.

Psychics visiting the apothecary all come away having sensed the presence of a warm, welcoming, and friendly spirit there. All similarly agree

Judge Campbell, born 1806

Some believe it is Judge Campbell, a powerful man whose offices were located in the building, who haunts the Niagara Apothecary.

that he is a distinguished gentleman who worked and perhaps resided in the building, but his identity remains unknown. Some sensitives suggest the ghost is that of a former pharmacist, but others thought he might be Judge Campbell, still holding court over his beloved town.[3]

Tim, who asked to remain anonymous, believes the latter to be the case. And his opinion should bear some weight in the matter, since it's based on eyewitness testimony. Tim is an avid ghost hunter, someone who attempts to capture evidence of the existence of spirits. He also believes he has medium abilities. It was during one of his investigations that he came face to face with the ghost of the apothecary.

"I didn't have real permission to investigate the building, so I couldn't really do anything inside. Instead, I decided to come by late at night and do an investigation of the exterior," explains Tim, who had hoped to channel someone from the past. He succeeded beyond his wildest dreams.

"I arrived at about two thirty in the morning, when the streets were completely empty. It was almost creepy, really, and immediately I began to feel the presence of an authority figure from within the building. I even heard a voice in my head that said, 'I am drunk. I need to speak.' But I have no idea what that means."

Encouraged by the strength of the connection, Tim pressed his face up to the front window of the apothecary. Shadows draped over the perfectly preserved nineteenth-century interior, making details almost impossible to pick out. He leaned closer, eyes straining, hoping to see something that would validate his feelings. Tim's screams of horror suddenly cut through the night's silence as he stumbled backwards from the window.

"Standing right on the other side of the window was a man with white curly hair wearing a formal black coat," says Tim. "When I calmed myself enough to investigate the spot where he was, no one was there. The building was empty again."[4]

But as so many have discovered over the years, even when the Niagara Apothecary appears empty, there's always someone present. But who exactly is this ghost? That's a question that has perplexed many. Even psychics can't agree. The one thing everyone seems to agree upon is that it's a male figure with a palpable sense of authority, someone who is used to commanding respect from those in his presence.

That could easily describe three prominent individuals connected to the apothecary. Judge Campbell, who held court in this building for many years, is the most obvious candidate. He was a stern man, used to getting his way; his word, quite literally, was law. Henry Paffard is another possibility. He was, after all, Niagara-on-the-Lake's longest serving mayor (a total of twenty-three years) and a gentleman who wielded considerable power.[5] And then there is John de Witt Randall, Paffard's successor as village pharmacist. Randall was mayor for one term, district deputy grand master of the Masonic Lodge, and a warden of St. Mark's Anglican Church. He was a beloved member of the community and exercised considerable influence over its affairs. His death was a black day; flags flew at half mast, businesses closed, and hundreds of citizens lined the route of the cortege. Is he the ghost who haunts the Niagara Apothecary?[6]

As so often is the case where paranormal phenomenon is concerned, we'll never know the answers to many of our questions regarding this historic building in Niagara-on-the-Lake. Hiding, lurking just out of sight and beyond normal senses, the spirit — whoever he is — waits for the most opportune time to reveal himself to the unsuspecting public.

9
OLD COURTHOUSE

Old buildings have strange stories to tell. The old courthouse, located at 26 Queen Street, has more than most. A national historic site and perhaps the most magnificent structure in Niagara-on-the-Lake, it has played host to cut-throat politics, trials involving heinous crimes, and even its share of chilling ghost stories. "This building has seen a lot of small-town drama over the years," says Ron Dale. "And I think some of that energy remains behind, including, perhaps, spirits."

The courthouse is actually the third in Niagara-on-the-Lake's history. The first was built in the early nineteenth century before the War of 1812 broke out, and it was located not far from the current courthouse. It was destroyed, along with the remainder of the town, when the occupying Americans retreated back across the Niagara River in December 1813. A replacement was built shortly after the war, but farther inland so that it was out of range of American artillery at Fort Niagara. This courthouse was in use for almost three decades, but by the 1840s the residents of Niagara-on-the-Lake began to plan for a new, more ambitious public building.[1]

It was all a matter of politics. At the time, and thanks to the prosperity afforded to it by the Welland Canal, St. Catharines was growing rapidly and challenging Niagara-on-the-Lake's position as the economic and political hub of the area. The people of St. Catharines looked to the future with confidence, and believed their community should be the seat of Lincoln

County, not Niagara-on-the-Lake. Their petition for the honour kick-started a bitter feud between the rival towns. Hoping to force the hands of government decision-makers, Niagara-on-the-Lake began construction of a large and expensive courthouse that would house judicial and clerical functions for the county. The current courthouse was the result.

Unfortunately, the plan didn't work as expected. In 1862, St. Catharines was named county seat, leaving the people of Niagara-on-the-Lake embittered and saddled with a massive structure that was now all but obsolete. In the aftermath of the decision, the building housed the county sheriff's office, the mayor's office, meeting chambers, council offices, a strongroom for locking up money, and holding cells for prisoners. It brought together Niagara-on-the-Lake's movers-and-shakers — men of power, prestige, and pride — under one roof, where they could chart the future of the community.

Some of these men, though long dead, refuse to give up the reins of leadership and continue to lord over the courthouse as if it were still their domain. To these spirits, it doesn't matter that the town halls have long-since moved, leaving the building to house only the Court House Theatre, the local chamber of commerce, and offices for Parks Canada.[2] They see the courthouse as it was in the nineteenth century, when it was a place of influence where they held the authority.

Ron Dale, who for many years had his office in the building, notes there were times when he felt some otherworldly spirit was keeping an eye on what was happening. He believes this spirit is none other than Judge Edward Campbell.[3]

"Edward Clarke Campbell was a judge of the United Counties of Lincoln, Welland, and Haldimand, and had his offices here in this building," Dale explains. "He was always complaining of the cold in this big, stone building and said it would be the death of him. Ironically, on January 18, 1860, he died of pneumonia at the age of fifty-four.

"I had my offices in the same room Judge Campbell would have had his offices. I always liked my room cold, so it never bothered me as it did the judge, and I always had the thermostat all the way down. Yet on several occasions I'd find the room getting uncomfortably hot and notice that the thermostat had been turned up really high. The only way it could have been turned up was by me, and I never touched it. I believe Judge Campbell was at work, trying to keep it warm in his old office."

Yet the presence of Judge Campbell in his office never made Dale feel uneasy. In fact, it made him feel closer to history. But the second floor where the Court House Theatre is located was another matter entirely. Here, he routinely got an odd feeling, as if someone was watching him with cold eyes. Interestingly, he isn't the only one to feel an unpleasant entity in this chamber.

"The courthouse was the Shaw Festival's original venue when it began back in 1962, and over the past fifty years people have grown fond of it because it's a very intimate theatre. Maybe some people are too fond of it, because some of our staff over the years have reported seeing ghosts there," says Megan Gilchrist, education coordinator for the Shaw Festival. "One of our managers used to see two figures walking near the stained glass window in the Court House Theatre. We don't know who they were in life, what connection they have to the building, or why they were only seen walking by the window. Also, bar staff often see a mysterious male figure in the hall. It definitely has energy." Cold spots have been felt, and soft, ghostly whispers and strange banging noises have been heard throughout the building, especially in the theatre. There are times when people feel malicious eyes boring into them from behind, but when they look, there is never anyone present. Occasionally, when you're the only one in the place, you can hear haunting footsteps. While they don't always originate from the second floor, those that do sound like heavy boots worn by someone striding with a purpose.

A one-time co-worker of Ron Dale, a fellow Parks Canada employee named Sharon, had a weird experience in the theatre. It was a few years back, sometime in early November after the Shaw Festival had closed up for the year. At that time, the upstairs was the only place in the building where you could smoke, so when Sharon and a co-worker decided to take a break from the monotony of work they headed for the now-empty theatre. A janitor was there at the time but he left shortly after they arrived, leaving the door ajar.

It was then that an unusual feeling came over Sharon, and she felt an icy-cold wind that caused goose bumps to form on her skin. Suddenly, the door slammed shut with terrifying force. The two women jumped with fright. It wasn't just the unexpected sound that had startled them, but the fact that there was no source for the icy wind that caressed their skin and slammed the door; no windows or exterior doors were open nearby. They raced down the stairs and out of the theatre, cigarettes unfinished.

The following account was shared with us by Daniel Cumerlato of Ghost Walks, a group that runs ghost tours in Niagara-on-the-Lake.[4] Though it may sound fantastic, we're assured it comes from a reliable source.

It's common knowledge among residents of Niagara-on-the-Lake that it's best to avoid being alone in the courthouse after 5:00 p.m. As early evening arrives, the building's cavernous interior becomes the domain of the restless dead, and they don't take kindly to intrusions. It's a foolhardy person who ventures into the courthouse by themselves at this time.

And yet, a cleaning lady ignored the warnings and remained behind after the building had closed at 5:00 p.m. She wanted to finish her work before going home, and wasn't going to let whispered warnings about ghosts keep her from her task. It was all just tall tales, she figured, and she wasn't about to be chased from the building like a frightened schoolgirl.

At first, all went well and the woman began to openly scoff at the chilling stories she'd heard so frequently. Then she found herself upstairs, cleaning a room with a large, ornate chandelier overhead. The woman noticed that the chandelier was swinging slowly back and forth, as if caught by the wind, even though there wasn't a noticeable air current in the room and no open doors or windows. Perplexing, but not yet frightening.

Then the chandelier began to pick up speed, swinging faster and faster, the glass rattling ominously and the light it cast dancing crazily across the room. The chandelier started shaking, as if there was an earthquake, but the floor and walls were still. At this point, the woman was wide-eyed and her legs rubbery with fear. As if torn from the ceiling by invisible hands, the chandelier suddenly gave way and came crashing to the floor right in front of the terrified woman, showering her with glass. It was clear that someone, or something, was angry with her and wanted her out of the building. She was all too happy to oblige, and raced from the building, never to return.

Others have had nerve-racking encounters with the unpleasant entity lingering on the second floor of the courthouse. One summer visitor was sent away shivering after being engulfed by an icy blast, and another heard a man cursing in an otherwise empty hallway. Who's responsible for these disturbing phenomena? While we can't pinpoint a specific person, many believe the answer lies in the relatively brief time the building served as a place of judgment.

Several trials took place in the courthouse between the time it was built in 1847 and the time such functions were moved to St. Catharines in 1864. Some of these trials broke the accused, leaving their reputations besmirched, their spirits crippled, and their wealth gone. Sometimes the guilty would be sentenced to lengthy jail terms in the notably inhumane prisons of the day. Many died before they could be paroled, while others emerged mere shells of their former selves, body and soul eroded by years of abuse. And in a surprising number of cases, and for what today seem like relatively minor offences, the accused were sentenced to the gallows.

Could it be that the spirit of someone tried and convicted here is the otherworldly presence lingering in the Court House Theatre? It would seem to explain the hostile nature of the wayward soul. It might also explain why some visitors report having seen the door of the reconstructed holding cell on the main floor — a door that is extremely heavy, one might hasten to add — slowly swing shut on its own, and why that cell is filled with such palpable malignancy.

A mother and her young daughter decided to walk through the old courthouse as part of their exploration of the countless historic buildings in Niagara-on-the-Lake. They had been impressed with the century homes, the quaint shops, and opulence of the Prince of Wales Hotel, but this imposing building touched them in a way none of the others did. They entered the courthouse tentatively at first, unsure whether it was actually open to the public. It was ominously quiet at the time; the building which would have been full just weeks prior during tourist season was all but empty, and their footfalls echoed through the cavernous halls.

Mother and daughter came upon the holding cell just off the grand hallway. Like most children, the daughter was intrigued by the chamber. Before her mother could stop her or scold her for running, the impetuous girl had pulled the heavy door open and stepped inside to investigate. Mother followed daughter to escort her out, but upon entering, pulled up short. She noticed her daughter was standing completely still, with a faraway look on her face. Then she heard it — a whispered voice that reached out from some dark day far in the past.

Mother and daughter are both sensitive to the dead. Neither is sure whether it's a gift or a curse, but both agree it's something they've learned to deal with. Usually, their sensitivity comes in the form of vague impressions, overwhelming déjà vu, sometimes unusual insight. Never had they actually communicated with a spirit, but that all changed in the oppressive darkness of the cell. Mother and daughter stood in silence, seemingly unable to break the connection with someone long dead who desperately wanted his story told. The spirit, a male with a heavy, rough voice, was speaking rapidly as if afraid his audience would leave before he had said his peace. The mother actually asked out loud for the entity to slow down so he could be understood.

Suddenly, a form began to materialize within the cell and a face peered out between the bars. Though it was dark, the man seemed to have sallow cheeks, an unkempt beard, bloodshot eyes, and teeth that were stained and grimy. He looked every bit the hardened criminal, a deserving prisoner, and the young girl let out a wail of fright that echoed through the hall as she ran for the doors and the comfort of sunlight outside.

The mother found her daughter sitting on a bench outside. She put a protective arm around her and hugged her close. "Mom," the girl asked at last, "that man scared me, was he dangerous?" The mother assured her that he wasn't, and that he couldn't hurt anyone anymore. The young girl chewed her lip in deep thought. Finally, after a few moments of silence, she asked, "Do you think he did it, Mom?"

Until that point, the mother wasn't sure how much her daughter had actually experienced within the cell, whether she had heard the ghost telling his story, whether the child even realized he was an apparition and not a flesh-and-blood prisoner. The ghost claimed he had been tried for something he didn't do, and kept repeating over and over again, "It was not me. Please hear me. I did not do it. Help me prove my innocence." Unfortunately, it was well past the time when that would do any good. The man had been convicted and sentenced to the gallows.

The crime had been so small, so inconsequential, that the mother found herself disbelieving that a man could even be tried for it. According to the spirit's own testimony, he had simply been walking alongside a more refined gentleman and happened to notice a billfold drop from the man's overcoat. He bent down to retrieve and return it, and was immediately accused — solely on the basis of his appearance — of trying to rob the gentleman. The next thing he knew he was in prison awaiting his trial.

The daughter had tears in her eyes when she looked up at her mother. "Not all poor people are thieves."

The mother agreed, and hugged her. "But you can't travel back in time to fix the past," she said. "That's just the way it was back then. Even the smallest of crimes had harsh punishment." It was small consolation, and the mother wished she could have shielded her daughter from the harsh realities of the world for a few more years at least.

There was nothing they could do for the ghost. He was beyond help; he had been tried and convicted, and his sentence carried out at the end of a rope. All they could do was step back into the courthouse and assure

The old courthouse is a true gem of nineteenth-century Niagara-on-the-Lake. It is also haunted by a restless prisoner and the judge who sentenced him to the gallows.

the poor man that they believed him and that they hoped one day he could find some peace. How many more people must believe in his innocence before the spirit can rest at last? We may never know. Perhaps for this restless soul there can be no commuting of the sentence, and he is condemned to an eternity trapped between two worlds.[5]

Opportunities to learn more about these spirits through face-to-face encounters will soon be more limited, explains Gilchrist. "Unfortunately, as of 2018 there will no longer be theatrical performances in the courthouse. It can be a challenge for people because getting to the upstairs theatre requires climbing a number of stairs. The Accessibility Act will be taking effect in 2020, and because the courthouse is a designated heritage structure, it's not practical to make it accessible. Instead, we'll be moving to another purpose-built venue, and the hall at the courthouse will be used only for rehearsals and as a space for talks," she explains.

The old courthouse is a treasured historical site, and in its cavernous halls, the recreated council chambers, and even in the oppressive confines of the holding cell, one can't help but feel as if time has stood still there. The building is a strangely intimidating place, and one swears the echoes of those whose lives were shaped, for good or bad, by the decisions made within its rooms can still be heard or felt.

Could these echoes, in fact, be real — the shades of people who have been unable to pass on to the afterlife, and remain trapped in this monument to a time long past? Many certainly believe so.

10
PILLAR AND POST INN

The Pillar and Post Inn incorporates a historical structure that was originally built in the late 1890s as a fruit canning factory. But despite its humble beginnings, the Pillar and Post happens to be Ontario's only five-star country inn. It's so beautiful, in fact, so hospitable and comfortable, that some guests simply didn't want to check out. But that's all right with the staff; they consider the resident ghosts to be as much a part of the inn's charm as its trademark indoor hot springs, the European-style 100 Fountain Spa, and the nostalgic warmth of the Cannery Restaurant.

The fruit industry, for which Niagara is well known, began in the late nineteenth century when canning technology emerged that enabled the export of locally grown fruit for distant markets. Factory 13, the building that today forms part of the Pillar and Post, was built in 1892 to process and can peaches and tomatoes. For over five decades, Factory 13 was among the largest and most efficient canning facilities in the Niagara Region. Even the onset of the First World War and the conversion of the upper floor into a supply storeroom for Polish soldiers being trained nearby didn't hinder its operation or put a cramp in its reputation for excellence.[1]

But while war couldn't affect the cannery, changing market conditions could, and by the 1950s Factory 13 was no longer competitive. It was closed in 1957 and the building sat vacant for a number of years before being reopened as a basket factory. In 1970, the building was converted into a restaurant and craft centre, and then in 1972 it was transformed into the Pillar and Post Inn, with a modest total of thirty-five guest rooms. There have been numerous expansions and ambitious renovations in the years since, and today the inn boasts 122 luxurious guest rooms, a top-of-the-line spa, and a restaurant that is consistently ranked as one of the finest in the region.[2]

It surely must also be ranked as one of the more haunted hotels in the region, with as many as four resident wraiths intent on revisiting their past in the cozy confines of this country inn. Guests are lured to the Pillar and Post by its reputation for outstanding hospitality, but they must be prepared to share their dinner table or accommodations with a ghostly companion. Unfortunately, the identity of these ghosts — the innocent little girl dressed in red, the mischievous ghosts of Room 118, and the foul-tempered entity

This is the image of the Pillar and Post that most guests are familiar with: warm and comfortable, the ideal place to spend a night or two. Few realize that ghosts lurk in the shadows of this historic building.

in Room 222 — remain just one of the many secrets that a building with more than a century of history must contain. The only spirit that has been identified is Lieutenant Colonel John Butler, his intimidating presence all but unmistakable.

The Cannery Restaurant is said to be the most haunted location within the nostalgic and comforting inn, and it's only here that any of the inn's ghosts ever manifest as a visible entity. One can imagine how staff and diners would be taken aback by the sudden materialization of a young girl among the tables, her simple, outdated dress so at odds with the refined setting. They're even more startled when she fades from sight a few seconds later, having never said a word nor done anything beyond merely gazing out at the restaurant with curious interest. One of the hallmarks of the Cannery are the large pillars throughout the dining area, and it's not at all uncommon for staff to walk around one of these pillars and pass through the ethereal girl standing behind it. On some occasions, the youngster — whom staff members at the Pillar and Post have named Laura — has been seen to walk through these supporting beams or to simply fade away into their wood grain.[3]

"It was late at night, approaching midnight on Halloween, when I saw a little girl standing beside the pillar right in front of the fireplace," remembers dining room supervisor Bill Putman, a level-headed and rational man. She was four feet tall and surrounded by a gold silhouette — the same colour as the flames in the fireplace. She was perfectly clear to me and remained for ten to fifteen seconds, growing brighter with each passing second, before fading off into the wood of the pillar. I've seen her four times since, always between eleven forty-five and midnight on Halloween."[4]

"The staff are fond of this little girl and see her a lot, often on the staircase just outside the restaurant," adds Shane Howard, the inn's front office manager. "She's dressed in red, comes down the stairs and sits on the landing halfway, but won't come all the way down. No one knows why she won't come down, and no amount of coaxing can convince her to."

Like any child, Laura is fond of playing practical jokes as well. One story that illustrates this precocious behaviour was submitted to the Toronto and Ontario Ghosts and Hauntings Research Society by an unidentified employee of Vintage Hotels, who stresses that the eyewitness to the tales was credible.[5]

An ethereal girl often appears before this very post in the inn's restaurant, slowly fading back into the woodwork moments later.

"One of the bussers in the dining room had forgotten her name tag and found one in the hostess stand, so she put that on for the evening," the source explains. "That night, she felt as if someone was pulling on her hair. She didn't think anything of it. She then felt as if someone was tugging on her shirt when she was climbing the stairs. She was serving a drink to a table, holding the drink on her tray, when all of a sudden the glass was knocked over. She had been completely still and the guests at the table also saw it, commented that it was weird it knocked over like that. The busser had said it felt like someone just knocked the tray from her hands."

In an eerie coincidence, it turns out the same thing happened to another waitress a few years earlier and unnerved her so much that she immediately quit. Ironically, it had been her name tag that the busser was wearing that night.

Sheri, a waitress at the Cannery Restaurant, was kind enough to tell us about her ghostly experience that took place in 2011. It was late in the evening, and she was waiting on one final table occupied by diners lingering over their meal. Sheri was looking forward to getting home so she could rest her tired feet, and was eager for this couple to finish their meal so she could complete her tasks and finally leave for the evening.

The diners eventually paid the bill and made their way out of the restaurant. A grateful Sheri started the task of getting her work area clean and ready for the next day. She was wiping down the table when she heard the chair behind her slide forward. "It sounded like someone was helping me by pushing in the chairs," she remembers.

Sheri turned to check on who was being thoughtful and to thank her helper, but to her surprise there was no one there. There were, of course other people elsewhere in the inn, but no one was left in the restaurant. At least, not anyone she could actually see. But the noise hadn't been a figment of her imagination, because a chair that minutes before was pulled away from its table was now inexplicably pushed in.

Even though an experience like this suggested someone unseen was in the same room, and might have left some people scared, Sheri felt no fear. Quite the contrary, she felt a warm and friendly presence, that of someone who was graciously helping her complete her tasks. She thanked the thoughtful spirit and went about her business.

The identity of the unseen spirit is unknown. Sheri seems to think it was an adult female, perhaps an employee of the old canning factory, and not Laura, the lonely little girl spirit she has heard so much about. But, of course, that's merely an impression.

What if the spirit was in fact Laura's mother, trying to reunite with her long-lost daughter? Perhaps a mother's love for her child transcends life and death? No one will ever know.

The adjacent lounge and bar is another paranormal hotspot. This cozy, fire-lit room is intimate and charming, the ideal place for a quiet glass of wine and a hushed conversation. Yet, despite the warmth of the hearth, some suggest there's something cold about the room, an intangible sense of lurking malice hiding just out of view. This chill seems to be centred on a painting of Lieutenant Colonel John Butler that hangs above a pair of comfortable chairs.

Folklore suggests this oddly unsettling painting was the Colonel's favourite portrait of himself, and that his spirit followed it to the Pillar and Post and often sits in the chairs beneath it. This is actually quite common; many ghosts are not tied to a specific location, but rather an object that had great personal significance to them, such as a favoured piece of clothing, heirloom furniture, the tools by which a craftsman made his living, or prized jewellery. It's therefore possible that Butler was so attached to this particular painting that, upon his death, his spirit clung to it as a means of remaining within the community he helped establish.[6]

Whatever the theoretical explanation, the fact remains that, according to Bill Putman, several members of the serving staff are actually afraid of Butler's painting. "They say they feel as if his eyes actually follow them as they walk through the room, and some servers have felt the hair on the back of their necks rise as if they could sense someone unpleasant watching them," he explains. "It's also said that temperatures sometimes change suddenly and drastically in the lounge, for absolutely no reason." The door just to the side of this painting is said to open and close on its own accord and people have inexplicably tripped in front of these chairs — as if stumbling over the invisible Colonel's outstretched legs. In addition, cutlery and plates are said to mysteriously move from table to table, much to the frustration of the staff.

Elsewhere, Rooms 118 and 222 are said to have a particularly active ghostly history.[7] The disposition of the spirits lingering in these rooms couldn't be more dissimilar. Some ghosts are vengeful entities. They might feel as if they should still be alive and are resentful of those with flesh and blood. They might also feel territorial of their surroundings and look upon any who venture into their space as unwelcome intruders. The ghost of Room 222 falls into this category — an ill-tempered spirit who just doesn't seem to like people.

Thankfully, other ghosts are far friendlier. They stay around because they enjoy the living world and don't want to part with it. These ghosts are either at peace with their undead status or oblivious to it, and therefore are rarely a problem for mortals. In most cases, they're happy to share a residence with the living. This is the case with the ghosts of Room 118, where pleasant, English-accented female voices can be heard coming from the room even when it's unoccupied. Most who experience this phenomenon agree there are two distinct voices, and that they sound elderly. Along with inexplicable conversation, the fireplace is known to light by itself, making the place cozy and comfy for whoever is present. These friendly female ghosts often amuse themselves by playing practical jokes with guests staying in the room. When sleeping, the ghosts will tug at your blankets, just to let you know they're present.

Music is another way that they try to connect with people, as a woman on the cleaning staff explains: "It was just before Christmas and I was tidying up Room 118. I knew that the room was supposedly haunted, but I never experienced anything, so it didn't bother me. The clock radio had been on when I came in and it was playing old-time sounding Victorian Christmas tunes ... you know, harpsichord stuff, which I enjoyed while doing my cleaning. I finished up and, as I left, I turned off the radio ... but the music continued to play."

At this point, the woman didn't think much of it. She continues with her story. "Assuming that there was some sort of electrical problem, I went to unplug it and plug it back in again. And the music continued to play, even though the plug dangled from my hand. I opened up the battery door to confirm that it was empty, and the music continued to play. I decided that this was a job for management, so I carried the battery-less, unplugged machine to my boss's desk ... and the music continued to play." By this point, the poor woman was nearly beside herself; a clock radio should not, by all rational reasoning, play without a source of power. And yet, the one in her hand was.

Returning together to Room 118, the woman and her boss replaced the radio by the bed and plugged it in once again. Then the boss, who clearly had experience with the playful haunts, addressed the room. "Okay, ladies," he said in a kind voice. "You can listen to the music, but I've got guests checking in, in forty-five minutes, so you need to shut it off by then." He then simply closed the door behind him and let the ghosts enjoy the holiday tunes a while longer. Later, when the room was checked just before the new guests arrived, the music had stopped playing.

In another incident, the ladies of Room 118 couldn't resist playing around with a young couple.[8] The guests, who were visiting from Buffalo and looking forward to a pleasant stay at the Pillar and Post, got more than they bargained for. Certainly, they had no idea they would have to share their accommodations with a pair of ghosts. One night during their stay, the young couple decided to go for a walk. Before leaving, they made sure to turn off the fireplace. Yet, when they returned a few hours later, the place was toasty warm with the fireplace roaring in the hearth, having mysteriously lit itself. Later in the evening, when they came back from a ghost tour of Fort George, the couple was startled to find the clock radio playing music, even though it had no snooze and the alarm had yet to go off. Settling in for a relaxing, cozy evening, they ordered room service and commented to their waiter about the unusual events. He didn't seem at all surprised and simply said, "I see the ladies are active today," before explaining about the resident ghosts.

Unfortunately, no one has any idea who these elderly ladies are or why they remain bound to the Pillar and Post. But while perhaps quirky, they're a harmless pair of old gals and are more than willing to share their bed with strangers.

In direct contrast to Room 118, Room 222 is said to be haunted by a less-than-friendly ghost who resents the intrusion of mortal guests into its domain. The list of unusual, occasionally even frightening, phenomenon that occur in this premium suite is extensive: doors are known to slam with terrible force; jewellery and other small items are stolen by otherworldly hands, sometimes turning up hours later, other times never reappearing; electrical appliances turn on and off of their own accord, often in the middle of the night, interrupting sound sleep; and objects are swept off tables by an unseen force.

Staff members at the Pillar and Post are long-acquainted with the haunts and horrors of this particular guest room. Shane Howard, the inn's front desk manager, for example, remembers an old rocking chair that would rock by itself, slowly creaking back and forth as if someone was sitting in it. Several cleaning ladies have experienced the sensation of invisible eyes boring into them, and have left the room in a hurry after the television suddenly flared to life or the impression of a body appeared in the line of a just-made bed.

Jeff, a doorman who was once an overnight security guard at the Pillar and Post, vividly recalls his own encounter with the unsociable ghost in Room 222. "One of my duties as a security guard was to walk the buildings and make certain all the guest-room doors were closed and secure," he explained. "It was around three o'clock in the morning on this one particular shift when I found Room 222 wide open and everything in there on. The fireplace was burning, every light was on, and the TV and radio were playing. I was a bit confused, but entered the room to turn everything off and secure the room. As soon as I stepped in, I got chills and the overwhelming feeling that I had to leave. It was like someone was telling me to get out — now. I turned off the lights and left immediately, not bothering to turn off anything else. I thought, 'The heck with it, everything can stay on until morning.' That experience really creeped me out, and I still remember the goose bumps it gave me." As with the ladies of Room 118, the identity of the resident spirit in Room 222 is unknown, and why it refuses to share the accommodations is anyone's guess. Why is he so possessive of the room that, on occasion, he'll chase people out with a combination of unsettling antics and oppressive atmosphere? What is the nature of his malice toward the living? We'll probably never know. Thankfully, the ghost is only occasionally active and most guests enjoy the comfortable suite without the slightest inkling that another patron, someone long-dead and now incorporeal, has requested a permanent extension of their check-out time. And with an inn so welcoming and appealing, who could blame the spirit for not wanting to leave?

Although the Pillar and Post is filled with modern amenities, its spirited past continues to filter through its rooms and corridors. In many cases this is intentional on the part of management, having succeeded in creating a property that effortlessly blends nostalgia and warmth with unmatched hospitality and the latest in comforts. In other instances, staff has little control over how or when the past — or more specifically, spectres who belong to the past — will intrude upon the modern. It's just part of the charm of the Pillar and Post.

11

CORKS RESTAURANT

Corks Restaurant carries on the proud tradition of being one of the oldest and most popular restaurants in Niagara-on-the-Lake. It's also believed to be among the most haunted dining establishments, due to a long string of paranormal activity that took place during the decades it operated as the Buttery. Ghostly activity has either died down in recent years or the present owners are more reluctant to speak of spectral matters; either way, most of the best stories emerged during the time the restaurant was known as the Buttery so that's where we focus our attention in this chapter.

As the Buttery, the ground floor was home to a traditional English-style eatery with a pub-style menu, and the second floor boasted the medieval King Henry VII dinner theatre, where patrons enjoyed a fine meal while being entertained by actors and musicians in fifteenth-century costumes. For almost forty years, the Buttery was a fixture in town, beloved by locals and tourists alike.

Few realize that the building was the site of a horrible tragedy that left two dead during a murderous rampage. Ghostly entities from that night of violence and terror are embedded in the walls like bloodstains, their spirits tormented by bitter memories and the violent manner in which they perished. Some people who dine within the restaurant can sense echoes of that terrible day in 1850.[1] A select few people leave having seen apparitions intent on revisiting their past within the cozy confines of this atmospheric restaurant.

In 1850, the home of Lloyd and Kate Burn stood upon the site, but it was a complicated and far from happy household. They had courted in the manner of the day, meeting under the watchful eyes of their elders, with Lloyd pursuing in a courteous manner and Kate remaining proper and somewhat aloof. Eventually, Kate came around to the notion of marrying Lloyd. Truth be told, she had few options. Her parents were dead and a young woman in those days had few prospects for taking care of herself. But before they became husband and wife, one little detail had to be resolved: who would look after her brother, Philip, a young man with a mental illness? Kate couldn't leave him to fend for himself, so she stipulated that she would marry Lloyd only if Philip could come and live with them.

Lloyd grudgingly accepted the terms, but he, too, had a condition. Philip could join them in the house as long as he stayed in the basement under lock and key. This strange and cruel arrangement was made because Philip was both schizophrenic and prone to seizures, a condition that, in the nineteenth century, would be considered embarrassing at best and in extreme cases a sign of demonic possession. Most people with such an illness would have been confined to the harsh and depressing asylums of the day, where patients were locked up like animals and treated worse. Kate couldn't bring herself to send Philip to such a barbarous place, so she accepted Lloyd's terms.

Though unusual, the arrangement seemed to work when the newlyweds began their life as husband and wife. Lloyd and Kate settled into married life easily. If Lloyd could sometimes be demanding and abusive, Kate was at least content with the security that came with living with a husband and knowing she would be near at hand if her brother took ill. But whereas Lloyd and Kate were satisfied with the direction their lives were taking, Philip was not. This was not the way to treat a human being, he thought, and with each passing day he grew more restless living in a locked room — a prison really — in the cold, dark cellar. On occasion, Kate, the loving sister, would convince her husband to let Philip out to join them in the main house, but such brief tastes of normalcy only tormented Philip more. He craved freedom, to experience things beyond the four walls of the cellar.

The Burn house was unassuming and modest, but for a young couple starting out, it was more than they needed, and even big enough to start a family if they chose to. Architecturally, it was little different from most of the homes in 1850s Niagara-on-the-Lake, and yet it stood out, gaining a dark reputation due to the strange occupants. To the townsfolk, having an adult living under lock and key seemed abnormal, and the mysterious basement dweller — only ever seen fleetingly through drawn curtains on the rare occasions he was allowed to leave the basement — became the subject of wildly imaginative stories and whispered innuendo. But strange though the arrangement might have been, for the members of the Burn household this was the only way they could all live under one roof.

One day, Philip somehow managed to free himself from the locked basement. He was in a delusional state when he escaped, his normally peaceful self transformed into a force of pure rage. He met his sister, who was carrying a bowl of soup up to Lloyd, on the staircase and lashed out at her. The hot soup spilled over her abdomen and legs, scalding Kate and causing her to scream in agony. The shrieking rang mercilessly within Philip's skull, intensifying the thunderous headache that assailed him during seizures. In pain and startled by the screams, Philip unthinkingly pushed his sister away. He hadn't meant to hurt her, but she tumbled down the stairs and her body crumpled at the bottom.

Kate lay clutching her stomach, tears streaming down her face as she began to pray for the child growing inside her. Only moments before she had been excited by the prospect of becoming a mother, and was looking forward to revealing the happy secret to her husband and brother. Now all she could do was cry and, between bouts of pain, pray for her baby.

Seeing his sister twisted at the bottom of the stairs and hearing her pitiful cries enraged Philip to the brink of insanity. He turned his anger toward his brother-in-law. In his delusional mind, Lloyd was to blame. He should have let Philip live like a normal human, instead of being imprisoned in the basement where Philip's seething resentment led to this violent eruption. Now, because of Lloyd, Philip believed, he had hurt the only person who really loved and cared for him. For that, he would get revenge. Reaching for a knife, Philip began to climb the stairs. With each step, his rage grew, thinking about his sister lying near death on the floor. Fear and sorrow fuelled his murderous impulses. Lloyd had barricaded himself in his room with a large dresser up against the door, but Philip could not be stopped. Wood splintered as he stormed through the door, and when he came face to face with his brother-in-law, nothing was held back. Lloyd had taken everything from him: his sister, his freedom, his sanity. He had to pay. Like a wounded animal, Philip was relentless in his assault. He drove the knife into Lloyd's flesh time and time again until his brother-in-law had fallen bloody and lifeless to the floor.

His rage abating, Philip returned to his sister's side. By this time, Kate was barely alive, and her eyes closed as if asleep. He held her in his arms and took her hand. It was warm to the touch, and he covered it with his own, gently cradling her small hand. Kate turned her head his way. Her eyes fluttered under the lids and she moaned softly. When her eyes opened, they were dull and lifeless. She tried to focus, found Philip's face, and smiled faintly.

"I'm going to have a baby, Philip," she whispered. "You're an uncle. We'll be a happy family. And if Lloyd can't change, you and I are going to leave and start anew." Then she gasped and the spark of life was suddenly extinguished from her eyes. Philip begged her not to leave him, but while she would have done anything for her brother, she could not resist the call of death.

Philip panicked. He ripped up floorboards from the basement, dug a pair of hasty graves in the hard-packed earth, and buried Kate and Lloyd. He sat by the graves, unsure what to do next; for the first time in his life he was alone. The grieving young man couldn't bring himself to leave Kate's side, and still hadn't moved two days later when he was struck by a massive seizure. He collapsed in convulsions and died next to his beloved sister.[2]

Or at least, that's one version (albeit the most popular) of the story. In another version, Philip was the father, a doctor by trade and the unhappy father to a physically disabled and sickly child. Philip was ashamed of his son, feeling that having such a malformed child reflected badly on him as a man and would tarnish his image as a doctor, so he kept the lad largely confined to an upstairs bedroom. His wife, however, doted on their son. This only served to anger the already resentful doctor, who felt her attention was misplaced and should have been focused on reinforcing his image as a successful professional. One day, the years of anger and resentment finally broke Philip. Seeking to rid himself of the source of his embarrassment, he stealthily climbed the stairs and proceeded to smother the child with a pillow. Just as the boy was thrashing, his wife appeared at the top of the stairs and saw the murder unfolding. Husband and wife struggled. She fell down the stairs, breaking her neck as she tumbled head over heels. Being the only doctor in the area, Philip easily covered up the crime by filling out death certificates saying his son had finally succumbed to his long-term illness and that his beloved wife had died of grief shortly after.

Who can say for sure which version is true? Psychics and staff, however, believe the former, and back up their assertion with weight of spectral evidence.

However the tragic deaths occurred, there are many people who believed that something of Kate and Philip have remained behind.[3] It wasn't long after talk of the tragic events of 1850 finally began to die down that people began noticing strange noises coming from the building in the middle of the night. These unusual sounds continue to this day: ghostly whispers are regularly heard throughout the building, and on at least one occasion staff have heard the sickening noise of someone falling down the stairs only to find no one lying at the bottom. Others speak of quiet sobbing in the dark corners of the basement or long, agonizing moans upstairs where Lloyd met his grisly and painful end.

Murder most foul lies in the deep past of Corks Restaurant, formerly known as the Buttery. The haunting echoes of that crime can still be heard within the building today in the form of ghostly footsteps and disembodied whispers.

"We came here thirty-five years ago and purchased the building, then a tavern known as the Thistle and Shamrock," explained Buttery owner Margaret Niemann in a 2008 interview. "The present building sits on the foundations of the 1850s home, which had burned down, and, while it's not particularly old, it was designed to look colonial and fit in with the historical character of Niagara-on-the-Lake. We didn't know anything about the ghosts when we bought the building, but we soon began to get an idea something unusual was going on."

The ghosts made their presence known gradually, slowly building up the intensity and frequency of their paranormal activity. At first, it amounted to an inexplicable noise here, a shadow moving there. But soon the activity became more obvious and more unsettling for the new proprietors.

"We started to hear noises, like music and talking, coming from upstairs. My husband would tear upstairs, but there was never anyone there. It went on like this for a while before I finally asked the previous owner about it," Margaret explained. "She wasn't at all surprised, and was wondering when I would get around to asking her about the ghosts. In fact, the noises we were experiencing were minor compared to what she went through. Some nights, even with the pub full of customers, a terrible banging sound could be heard from upstairs. It was so bad that she was sure she was going to lose all her customers. There was never an explanation, and building inspectors could find nothing that would cause the noises."

That was just the first in what would be a continuous stream of spiritual activity that continues to this very day. Staff members insist they routinely feel watched by unseen eyes and see shadowy figures moving about in the corner of their vision.

The upstairs banquet hall where the King Henry VIII Feast played out was a hot spot for the Buttery's paranormal phenomena. Lights turned on and off by themselves, the dumbwaiter doors opened of their own accord, furniture moved as if by unseen hands, and sometimes, after the lights had been turned off for the night, staff members tripped over chairs that somehow found themselves pulled away from tables and into their path. Even those who were skeptical about the existence of ghosts occasionally found themselves looking over their shoulders when alone on the second floor, feeling as if someone — or something — were standing behind them.

A woman who, in the 1980s, performed the coveted role of the tragic Jane Seymour in the Henry VIII feasts shared some of the paranormal activity witnessed by staff during her employment. "Colleagues often complained that the ladies staff toilets would flush suddenly while they were still seated. Others had a problem with those 'back stairs' (the stairs leading to the second floor dining hall). The lights would reportedly go off, which was a bit dangerous, as most staff would be coming up the stairs balancing loaded trays, or others even reported having trays knocked out of their hands. The only phenomenon which I experienced was that music would suddenly come on mid-feast, even though the music booth was locked and the stereo turned off."

Naturally, she and many of her co-workers were quite alarmed. When they approached Margaret Niemann about their concerns, they were shocked to learn that things had actually been *worse* at one time. They learned that sometime before, Margaret, growing increasingly exasperated and frightened by the ongoing hauntings, had agreed to a seance in an attempt to contact who or whatever was haunting the building and maybe, just maybe, rid them of the spirit once and for all. Spectral activity had quieted measurably afterwards, but if the goal was to cleanse the building of spirits, the seance was clearly a failure — dozens of staff, Jane Seymour included, can attest to that.

One night, a staff member found herself cleaning up after a performance of the medieval dinner theatre. She was alone upstairs, focusing on her task and completely unconcerned, when an invisible hand slapped her back hard enough to produce a yelp of pain. Terrified, she raced downstairs to the comfort of her co-workers. When her shirt was lifted, a large, hand-shaped red welt was discovered on her back. No one could explain this violent outburst from ghosts that are generally mischievous but peaceful.

"Another time, two waitresses were folding napkins in the theatre. They weren't up there long enough to finish the job when they came down white-faced," remembered Margaret. "They saw a man dressed in old-fashioned clothes, who neither of them recognized, walk in one door and out another without even opening them. He simply passed through the doors, as if they didn't exist. Understandably, they were pretty shaken."

The basement runs a close second only to the second-floor when it comes to strange happenings. People report feeling uncomfortable down there, particularly the men's bathroom, where toilets will flush by themselves and disembodied male voices can be heard, as well as in the kitchen. Once, several people watched in terror as a plate floated off a pile of freshly washed dishes and flung itself across the room, shattering into pieces upon impact with the wall. On another occasion, Margaret and her daughter saw a man in a green coat entering the basement cold room where foodstuffs are stored. Following, they pulled open the heavy door, expecting to be confronted by the stranger. Instead, they found the room empty, as if the man had simply faded away.

Everyone agrees that the entity that haunts the restaurant's basement and theatre is Philip, and as far as Margaret was concerned, he was more than welcome to stay. "Everyone likes Philip, and we always make sure to say goodnight to him," she said. "I don't know what he did in his life, but he does no harm to us. Maybe he's trying to make up for what he did wrong in life."

Like her brother, Kate found little peace after her tragic death; her spirit lingers mostly near the staircase where she tumbled to her death. The lights on these stairs have been known to suddenly flicker and turn off, leaving wait staff to grope their way through darkness while balancing loaded trays. Other times, trays have been knocked out of their hands, spilling food and drink on the stairs. It's said that soup spills and burns are unusually common here; even Margaret suffered such an accident, badly scalding her legs.

Most spectacularly, an elusive woman was occasionally spotted on the staircase. She wore an old-fashioned dress, and there was an ethereal nature to her movements. Witnesses were left with no doubt that they had seen Kate, perhaps reliving the final moments before the fateful fall. It's uncertain whether the forlorn woman continues to linger within the restaurant's walls, however, because in the early 1980s, an exorcism was held that some believe allowed Kate to find peace. Others are adamant that Kate has been sensed and sighted with some frequency in the two decades since.

People who have witnessed the strange hauntings of Kate and Philip swear that both of their despondent souls continue to exist within the walls of the restaurant to this day. The brother and sister, who refused to be parted in life, remain united in death.

12
MCFARLAND HOUSE

John McFarland shuffled on unsteady legs along the country lane, his once-vigorous health undermined by almost two years as a captive of the American army. Before the enemy had thrown him in shackles and led him away to a prison camp in New York State, McFarland considered himself in fine health. There were the odd aches and pains, hardly unusual for a man of sixty-one years, but he could still pride himself in the ability to work in the fields alongside his sons, and had the upright walk of a far younger man. Now, with the war over, he felt old for the first time. His body was stooped and frail, his hands trembled, and walking was now a chore rather than a pleasure. McFarland felt tired.

He slowly made his way down the road, stopping frequently to catch his shallow breath. Though it had only been a few years, and he had passed this way hundreds of times before, McFarland barely recognized his surroundings. Orchards had been cut down to supply armies with firewood, farm fields had gone fallow after seasons left untended, and homes and barns had been burned by a vengeful enemy. The beautiful landscape McFarland had fondly thought back to during so many days of captivity was no more. What was left was a brutal scar.

McFarland continued on, eager to see his home again, and yet afraid of what he would find. He knew his beloved home, where five of his children had been born and where he had spent the happiest days of his life, had been used as a hospital during the conflict, so he held out hope that it had been spared from destruction. Sadly, it hadn't. When at last the home came into view, it wasn't the magnificent building of memory, a house envied by everyone in Niagara-on-the-Lake. It was little more than a roofless shell, the interior open to the elements and littered with the detritus of war, its furnishings vandalized by spiteful American soldiers. McFarland ran a calloused hand over watery eyes, unable to contain his emotions. It seemed everything he held dear — both of his wives, his youth, and now the home he had built with his own hands — had been snatched from him. It was devastating, and he was too old, too tired, to start again.

At that moment, McFarland lost the will to live. He became mired in misery, refusing to allow himself another chance at fulfillment. Less than a year later he would be dead of a broken heart. Niagara-on-the-Lake lost a founding father and a prominent, much-respected member of the community. Though he had not been slain by a musket ball, impaled by a bayonet, or swept away by artillery fire, he was just as much a victim of the War of 1812 as any of the thousands of soldiers who fell on either side.

McFarland House is one of the few homes in Niagara-on-the-Lake to survive the War of 1812. It was scarred by the conflict, though, and strange occurrences are reported there.

All this happened more than two hundred years ago, but John McFarland's spirit — made restless by the sadness of his final days and unwilling to be separated from the home that represented so many of his hopes and dreams — did not find peace. He is said to remain behind in his former home, now a museum operated by Niagara Parks as an example of the gracious residences found in early Niagara. Ironically, he may share the beautifully restored home with the very people who ruined it and sent its owner to an early grave; several people have reported seeing American soldiers wandering the building and grounds, presumably men who died there while it served as a military hospital.

McFarland House has stood from almost the time that Niagara-on-the-Lake was founded in the late eighteenth century. It was restored by the Niagara Parks Commission in 1959 to portray life in Niagara between 1800 and 1840, and to bring to life a home typical of those built by prosperous Loyalist settlers.[1] Since McFarland House is one of the few buildings to survive the American razing of the community in December 1813, it witnessed the full horror and suffering of the war. Little wonder then that McFarland House is heavy with the scent of history and folklore.

John McFarland was born in Paisley, Scotland, in 1752. He was a widower with four children when he immigrated to Niagara in the early 1790s. On December 31, 1798, McFarland received more than six hundred acres of land from King George III in reward for his services as a boatbuilder for His Majesty's forces.[2] He later purchased additional lots and was among the largest landholders in the vicinity. McFarland married Margaret Wilson, a neighbour in Niagara-on-the-Lake, and, with the assistance of his now-adult sons, built a fine manor home in 1800.[3] The house was designed to impress friends and neighbours, solidify his status as a leader in the community, and accommodate his growing family (which by the time Margaret died in 1809 included five additional children).[4]

In the summer of 1812, just a few short months before the American declaration of war and subsequent invasion of Canada, McFarland was a happy man. True, his second wife had passed away a few years prior, but he was wealthy, held in high esteem within the community, and had a fine home to serve as a symbol of his success. He counted himself lucky to have nine children, to be in good health, and to possess bountiful farmland and a profitable brick factory. Life was good for John McFarland, and one can imagine him spending quiet evenings in his den reflecting on how lucky he was.

Then the war came, shattering his idyll and ruining all he had built. John was over sixty and deemed too old for service in the militia, but he was caught up in the conflict nonetheless. In the summer of 1813, the Americans captured Niagara-on-the-Lake and sent the British defenders reeling inland. Shortly thereafter, John McFarland found himself arrested by the enemy and sent — along with other senior men of the community — to a prison camp in Green Bush, New York. Though beyond military age, the Americans considered these men a threat if left unattended behind their lines.[5]

To add insult to injury, the Americans threw the McFarland family out of their home and occupied it as a hospital for their sick and wounded. At times "the hall was sometimes so filled with the dead and wounded that it was almost impossible to reach the upper storey without treading on their bodies."[6] Many of these fallen soldiers never recovered from their grievous wounds; their blood stained the building's wood floors and their bodies were placed in unmarked graves on the property.

When John McFarland was repatriated at the end of the war in 1814, he returned to a home devastated by war. The roof, all interior wood-work (mouldings, banisters, and mantle pieces), and furnishings had been burned for firewood. All personal effects had been either stolen or destroyed. Windows were broken, dried leaves gathered in corners, and several seasons of rain and snow had damaged flooring, plaster walls, and expensive carpeting. The litter of war — bloodied bandages, empty packs, discarded uniforms — lay everywhere. Outside, the brickwork was crumbling, the paint had begun to weather and peel, and weeds consumed the gardens that had once blossomed with colourful flowers.

McFarland felt like his dreams had been shattered. Even after the roof was repaired and the home made habitable, McFarland could not escape his despondency. His mental and physical health deteriorated, and he retreated into the darkened bedroom of the home he had once been so proud of. He died a few months later from the heartbreak at the age of sixty-three. John McFarland was buried next to his wife at St. Mark's Cemetery at the foot of a headstone that relates his dying misery.

The gravestone of John McFarland, located in St. Mark's Cemetery, relates how he died of a broken heart after seeing the destruction of his home at the hands of American occupiers.

The sudden, tragic nature of his death and the words on his tombstone suggested from the beginning that the heartbroken man might not find peace in the grave. Local children, avid storytellers, ghost hunters, and a handful of eyewitnesses continued to build on the legend that McFarland House was heavily haunted. They reported unusual lights in the windows after dark, unnatural cold spots and chilly breezes without identifiable sources, and mysterious hushed voices and footsteps in the lower part of the home. Does this peaceful home mask a legacy of sadness that manifests itself in ghostly activity? Some believe so. Those who have experienced unusual activity there claim to know so. You be the judge.

"I saw a tall, elderly looking man wearing what seemed to me period costume, so I assumed he was a staff member," relates a woman who had an unusual experience during a visit to McFarland House. "He was reaching out to the mantle above the fireplace, as if placing something there. I only saw him from the back, and only for a moment, before turning my attention back to the tour group. When I glanced back again a second or two later, the old man was gone. It happened too fast for him to have walked through the other door. It was as if he just vanished. But he must have been there because crystal ornaments that rest on the mantle were tinkling ever so slightly, as if rustled by the wind." This woman was left convinced she had seen, if only momentarily, the ghost of John McFarland himself.[7]

Martha worked at the historical site for a number of years and was entirely positive that there was something, or someone, in the building besides mortal guides and tourists. While conducting tours, she was always hesitant to enter one particular second-floor room because, immediately upon crossing the threshold, the air would be sucked from her lungs, leaving her breathless and gasping. It would take a few seconds to recover, and she had to do it without alarming the members of the tour. She couldn't explain the breathlessness, and it was only in that one room that it ever occurred. Was this the room in which McFarland spent his final days and took his last breaths? Is it possible that Martha was experiencing a kind of echo of the heartbroken man's death, that her breathlessness reflected the air escaping his lungs as he slipped away? It's impossible to say.[8]

It's also impossible to say whether John McFarland does, indeed, remain in residence within the home he built so many years ago. If he does, one wonders how he co-exists with the undead American soldiers that lore says also inhabit this heritage building. After all, these men-at-arms represent the very people who imprisoned McFarland, destroyed his home and his health, and sent him to an early grave. It's probably an uneasy existence, but because they died here, either painfully succumbing to grievous wounds or feverishly wasting away due to illness, these spectral soldiers have as much claim to haunt McFarland House as does its builder; in the world of ghosts and spirits, deeds and ownership matter little.

The truth is that we have no idea exactly how many men may have died there, or where they are buried. Even Rebecca Pascoe, manager-curator of the site, doesn't have these answers. "I'm afraid that I cannot absolutely confirm or deny this ghostly tale," she told us honestly. "However, since the house was being used as a military hospital, and logic would dictate that not all patients survived their wounds, then yes, it is possible that soldiers died here and are, in fact, buried on the property."[9]

Those who have seen or felt these blue-coated spirits need no documentary proof to tell them that one or more American soldiers continue to occupy the building and the grounds, just as they did throughout 1813. Their senses are all the evidence they need. These men reach out from beyond the grave to ensure we don't forget that fallen warriors that lay beneath the ground where children play and families enjoy restful picnics. Unremembered and dead before their time, the ghosts still wander among the parkland and around McFarland House. Some people claim they appear in good health, tall and straight-backed, muskets at the ready, while others witness only bloodied and battle-weary soldiers.

McFarland House itself is not off-limits to the ghost soldiers. One witness heard terrifying moans of pain emanating from within the house during the off-season when the building was closed, while a medium who explored the building had sudden insight that made her certain that three people had been buried near the front wall in the basement and that perhaps five others were buried on the grounds. She also sensed that the basement was full of wounded, "like a hospital."

The most fantastic tale to come from McFarland House centres on a boy recovering from tonsillitis in the early 2000s. Complications had arisen from the normally routine surgery, leaving Jack Colgan feverish and bedridden for more than a week. Finally, the fever broke and he began to recover. The next few days passed slowly as boredom and inactivity took over. His strength returned quickly and Jack's parents felt that he was well enough for a day trip to Niagara-on-the-Lake. They thought getting out of the house would do him good, and hoped that the experience would cheer him up.

It was a warm and sunny May afternoon. The Niagara River gleamed, birds celebrated the new summer with song, and the air was softened by the new foliage that was emerging everywhere. Jack's mood brightened considerably, his recent illness forgotten in the excitement of the day. McFarland House was on the itinerary, and while he had been enthusiastic about visiting the old home as described by his parents, as soon as they pulled up to the elegant manor he felt ill at ease. Jack couldn't place it. On the surface the building seemed welcoming, but something gnawed at him nonetheless. It wasn't fear, but a type of despondency and sadness that he hadn't experienced before.

As soon as the guided tour started, Jack realized what was bothering him. The building felt like the hospital he had just left. There was that same grave atmosphere, that unmistakable sense that lives were hanging delicately in the balance. But that didn't make any sense; this was a beautiful, stately home, filled with wondrous antiques and, undoubtedly, happy memories. Nevertheless, the longer Jack was in the building, the more certain he was that dying people — not singly, but in large numbers — had once languished in the building.

He believes he saw one of the dead, as well. At one point his eyes happened to wander back to the room the tour had just vacated. There, standing grim and silent, was a cadaverous man in uniform with an angry glow flickering through the sockets of his eyes. In the time it took Jack to blink,

Stepping into the gracious confines of McFarland House transports you back in time to the early nineteenth century. Adding to the authenticity are spectres of the past, which may include John McFarland himself.

the vision was gone. But the fear that gripped the young boy would not dissolve so quickly. Almost two decades later, Jack is uncertain what to make of his experience. On the one hand, to his young mind it had seemed so vivid it could only be real. But as an adult, he's reluctant to admit to himself that he saw a ghost or felt the spirits of long-dead soldiers. Surely, only kids believe in ghosts. Jack believes it's possible that his youthful imagination, fuelled by stories fed to him by his parents and by the lingering effects of his recent illness, may have conjured up the whole episode. On the other hand, if other people experienced similar things in the building, couldn't it all have happened just as he remembers it?[10]

It's the mystery of not knowing for sure that makes ghost stories so engrossing. Thousands of people visit the beautifully restored McFarland House every year. They enjoy the experience of stepping back in time to an era when our nation was young, and through a guided tour learn the fascinating history of the building and the people associated with it. Many linger to sample refreshments at the McFarland House Tea Room. Only a tiny handful of those who visit this living history museum ever experience anything unusual or paranormal. And yet for many the possibility that they might make an intimate connection with the past by seeing or sensing a ghost — whether it's John McFarland himself or an obscure American soldier — seems to add to the building's charm.

Whether one believes in ghosts doesn't really matter. Neither does the truth behind whether McFarland House's tradition of hauntings is fact or fiction. What does matter is that these gripping stories, legends, and eyewitness accounts alike, real or imagined, are born of our fascination with the rich history associated with this unique Niagara attraction.

13

BUTLER'S BURIAL GROUND

Lieutenant Colonel John Butler, the man credited with founding Niagara-on-the-Lake, was a man of contradictions. Rarely has there been a soldier as loved and hated at the same time. To Canadians, he is a hero of immense proportions, a patriot who fought bravely and with notable success on behalf of the British Crown during the American Revolution, and who later helped lay the foundations for Niagara-on-the-Lake. To people south of the border, he is a traitor and a murderer, a man who turned his back on his country and, at the head of his Rangers, sought, through the most violent of means, to suppress the virtues for which his fellow Americans rose up in rebellion. The real John Butler was probably somewhere in between, neither angel nor devil.

Sadly for his legacy, Butler was caught up in a war that revealed the most brutal of humanity's behaviour, and he became defined — damned, even — by the actions he and his men took in the name of the Crown. On November 10, 1779, during the American Revolution's fourth year, a company of Butler's Rangers engaged in a punishing raid upon Cherry Valley, New York, in retaliation for the destruction of two British-allied Haudenosaunee villages by American colonial troops. The Rangers and their Haudenosaunee allies fought like rabid dogs and cut a bloody swath through the village, killing men, women, and children. After the slaughter, Butler's men took to the woods and raced away from the column of smoke that announced the consequences of their raid far and wide.

A legacy of hate was born in the moments when Butler's ruthless men overpowered and gutted the community. This outrage, known to this day as the Cherry Valley Massacre, left a dark stain on the name of all involved, and it condemned Lieutenant Colonel Butler — even though he wasn't present during the atrocity — in the eyes of many. In fact, these ruthless men were considered so vile that legend says that when they died of old age years later in Niagara-on-the-Lake, the ground they were committed to would not have them; their coffins were thrust out of the earth within months of burial, as if it could not digest such foul-tasting souls. As a result, their spectres, restless and haunted by the crimes committed centuries ago, remain behind long after the mourners have gone. Visitors to Butler's Burial Ground, the obscure cemetery where their bodies lay, have been startled by a wide range of terrifying supernatural phenomena.

The hauntings, the cemetery, and the blood-soaked Rangers all trace their origins to one man: John Butler.

The tombs that hold the bodies of the fallen soldiers of Butler's Rangers have been buried since this photo was taken a century ago to protect them from vandalism. Yet even this hasn't prevented the restless dead from wandering the cemetery at night or reliving a nearby War of 1812 skirmish.

John Butler was born in New London, Connecticut, in 1728, the son of Lieutenant Walter Butler and Deborah Ely. While still a young child, his family moved to the Mohawk Valley of New York State, which was then the frontier of colonial America. John was raised during the turbulent years of the Seven Years' War, and followed his older brothers into service in the British Indian Department, where he saw action in several battles.[1]

In 1752 he married Catherine Bradt, who came from a prominent Dutch family. Within a few years he had accumulated an estate of 26,600 acres valued at over 13,000 pounds, making him one of the wealthiest men in the Mohawk Valley.[2] Sadly, he lost it all — his home, his lands, and his wealth — as a result of the American Revolution and his decision to remain loyal to King and Country.

At the outbreak of the war in 1775, forty-seven-year-old Butler volunteered his services to Britain and was sent to Niagara to manage the Indian Department there. His two eldest sons, Walter and Thomas, accompanied him, but his wife and remaining children were taken captive by the rebels. Butler led a force of warriors to victory at the Battle of Oriskany in New York on August 6, 1777. This success led British commanders to urge Butler to raise an elite corps of Rangers to serve alongside the First Nations warriors and to fight in their style. This unit came to be known as Butler's Rangers, and would engulf the frontier in the horrors — raids, ambushes, and atrocities — of guerrilla warfare.[3]

A pattern of bloody campaigns along the frontier followed, with the Rangers emerging from the darkened depths of the forest to put villages to the torch, destroy crops, defeat rebel forces, and instill crippling terror in the enemy populace. Butler's Rangers became so notorious for their ruthlessness that when the conflict ended with an American victory, there was little hope of reconciliation between former enemies. They could never return home. Almost to a man, the men of Butler's Rangers packed up their families and headed for British protection in Niagara to establish new lives.

John Butler became a leader of the refugee community and, in fact, was so prominent and highly regarded that the young village (which one day would evolve into Niagara-on-the-Lake) was named Butlersburg in his honour.[4]

Butler died on May 12, 1796, after a long illness. He rests alongside family and fellow Rangers in a small, rural cemetery known today as Butler's Burial Ground.[5] It's a place with a long tradition of hauntings and unusual phenomena, suggesting one or more of the bodies interred there do not rest peacefully.

Butler's Burial Ground is located at the end of a wooded track on the outskirts of town. Even from a distance it radiates a noticeable aura of despair and decay. The cemetery stands atop a small hill and is surrounded by a dense wood of twisted trees. In the pre-dawn gloom and under the fading light of day, foul mists sometimes rise and curl above the grey ground. From somewhere in the distance a muffled cry or moan is heard — or perhaps it's only the wind.

Kyle Upton, author of *Niagara's Ghosts*, considers this to be one of the spookiest places in Niagara-on-the-Lake. Many locals agree, citing both its spooky atmosphere and the fact that disembodied voices and cold shadowy presences are frequently experienced here.

Cemeteries are places of remembrance, but perhaps that's the problem, the reason why Butler's Burial Ground is cursed to this day. The spirits who linger here would like to have the innocent blood washed from their hands and their consciences cleared of the atrocities they participated in, but it's not to be. With each visitor who wanders around the headstones and reflects on the lives of those interred here, the restless souls are reminded of their grievous crimes and how history has judged them. They feel guilt and sorrow. And these spirits remember as well how they were betrayed by the British decision to hand New York State over to the Americans at the end of the American Revolution, leaving them homeless and impoverished. Many of Butler's Rangers died embittered and resentful.

It's possible they are also embittered and resentful because of the way their graves were neglected. By the late nineteenth century, the fences around the burial ground had been removed, the plots overgrown, and cattle allowed to roam between the graves. Local historian Janet Carnochan noted that "the stones were found lying in all directions, broken by the fall of an immense tree which had been cut down, the vault fallen in and open to the inquisitive and irreverent gamine who has been known to carry off bones which should have been safe from such desecration."[6]

Awash in powerful negative emotions, it's little wonder that Butler's Burial Ground has acquired more than its share of eerie and paranormal stories. Whispers of ghosts and spirits walking the cemetery and its surroundings have long circulated through Niagara-on-the-Lake. Many claim to see misty glowing figures floating among the weathered and worn tombstones, and hear mysterious, chilling sounds that have no discernable source. Orbs are frequently captured on film, and an EVP recorded by John Savoie picked up voices saying, "Maybe we can go to heaven."[7]

At one time there was a stone crypt within the cemetery belonging to the Claus family, one of whom served in Butler's Rangers during the American Revolution.[8] The crypt was partially destroyed a century ago when a large tree fell on it, leaving the interior open to the elements and the bones exposed for desecration. Until recently, it served as a magnet for local teenagers eager for nighttime thrills and amateur ghost hunters. Many of these eager visitors found their enthusiasm crushed by an unmistakable terror that leaked out from behind the stone door sealing the tomb. There were coils of black smoke, an unnatural chill, and a host of unnatural sounds — banging and knocking, conversations, angry yelling, and even what sounded like fingers clawing at the inside of the door. Understandably, most of the would-be ghost hunters fled in terror soon after.

Nick (who asked that his full name not be revealed) was one person whose courage failed him during a midnight exploration of Butler's Burial Ground. His experience at the cemetery that night would leave him bewildered for years.

"I went late at night with a bunch of high school friends. As we got close to the cemetery I found my mind going back in time, but I'm not sure why," he explains. "There was something intangible about the chill I suddenly felt creeping along my spine, something I couldn't put a finger on, but it wasn't the cold."

Nick slowed his pace as he got closer to the cemetery, each step seemingly bringing him closer to some imperceptible evil. He stopped at the fence surrounding the grave site, suddenly unwilling to proceed. Even the taunts of friends questioning his bravery couldn't convince him to go farther. That's when he saw the figure looming in the shadowed entrance to the crypt.

"He was grey … I couldn't make out any features, but I could feel evil eyes boring into me," Nick says. "I felt threatened even though it just stood there, not moving. Then a wind picked up and, weird as it sounds, seemed to blow the figure away, just like the wind would blow away smoke."

His mind raced with all sorts of questions. Had he really seen a ghost? Or was he imagining it? If it was an apparition, was it one of Butler's men? He couldn't be sure. He still isn't sure.

Many others have been left equally confused. They report seeing a ghost standing in utter silence within the depths of the darkened cemetery, staring straight ahead, unmoving, dead-eyed, and cold. As witnesses watch, they experience an overwhelming sensation of steady and growing sadness. It's as if they are connecting with the true tragedy and loss of war: lost homes, shattered dreams, crippling wounds, emotional scars that refuse to heal, and innocence lost.

Yet according to some, the war that cost the dead so much has never truly ended. Indeed, given the sights and sounds that are reported around the old cemetery to this very day, more than a few of these old soldiers have remained there long after the call of duty expired.[9]

The men and women buried in Butler's Burial Ground led lives full of upheaval and trauma, but if they thought they would find some sort of peace upon their deaths they would be mistaken. They can't find any solace; the disembodied spirits and souls of the dead can find no rest.

14

SARAH ANN AND OTHER FORT GEORGE GHOSTS

No visit to Niagara-on-the-Lake is complete without a tour of Fort George National Historic Site. This venerable fortification played a vital role in the defence of Niagara-on-the-Lake during the War of 1812, and was all but destroyed in the fighting. Today, Fort George is comprised of several buildings — barracks, officers' quarters, and craftsmen shops — which have been designed to recreate the site as it would have been when Canada and the United States were at war. With costumed staff playing the role of military personnel and their families, passing through the fort's gates is like stepping two centuries back in time.

But the fort's palisades and earthen parapets contain more than just historical re-enactors and recreated buildings. These walls also enclose one of the most haunted places in Canada, a location so rich in paranormal activity that an entire book could — and indeed has — been written on the subject.

Kyle Upton has come to intimately know the various ghosts that inhabit the fort. For the past twenty years Kyle, the owner of Niagara Ghost Tours, along with members of his black-caped staff, has been escorting wide-eyed tourists through Fort George, with only lanterns to guide them through the darkness toward possible encounters with restless apparitions.[1] So many of these tours have resulted in unusual experiences that Upton was inspired to record the stories in two books. "There's an unusual amount of ghostly activity in the fort. Powerful, emotional experiences happened here — including fighting and devastation during the War of 1812 — and that taints the area, staining the earth with that psychic residue," he explains. "Fort George is probably the most haunted place in all of Niagara, with many ghosts and dozens of sightings over the years, and I believe much of this paranormal activity is the result of the fort's troubled past."[2]

In 1794, the terms of Jay's Treaty gave Britain two years to remove all its soldiers from the eastern (or American) side of the Niagara River. In accordance with that treaty, in 1796 the British garrison at Fort Niagara marched out of their fortifications and crossed over into Canada. Over the next three years, at a location just outside of Niagara-on-the-Lake, on a rising bluff overlooking the river, they built a replacement fort intended to control traffic on the Niagara River and protect the border from American attack. This fortification was Fort George.[3]

Fort George was the main base of the British forces in Upper Canada and was built within a large hexagonal earthwork with six earth-and-wood bastions and several blockhouses, with an outside ditch and a stockade enclosing the works. The fort's spacious interior contained a number of structures, including an officer's mess, three barracks, a guardhouse, and a stone powder magazine.

On June 18, 1812, the United States declared war on Britain with the intent of capturing Canada. For the first year of the conflict, Fort George remained largely unscathed by the fighting, but that all changed in the spring of 1813. On May 25, hundreds of American cannons opened fire on Fort George from across the river as the prelude to an invasion of Upper Canada (Ontario). A hail of incendiary shells rained down on the fort's wooden buildings, causing them to burst into flame, and by the next day Fort George had been reduced to a smouldering ruin. Only one building, the stone powder magazine, remained standing. Two days later, under the cover of a thick fog, American boats began to land on the shores of Lake Ontario, just north of the fort. British and Canadian defenders hotly contested the landing, but the sheer weight of numbers and overwhelming artillery fire caused the defenders to retreat. Niagara-on-the-Lake, and Fort George with it, fell into enemy hands.[4]

That winter, American forces were compelled to retreat by an advancing British army to their side of the river, but because its location had proven so vulnerable to attack, the British made no attempt to rebuild the shattered fort.[5] Instead, the British moved their military facilities to the less vulnerable Butler's Barracks and Fort Mississauga. Even after the War of 1812 ended with the Treaty of Ghent on February 17, 1815, the British showed little interest in returning to Fort George due to its proximity to Fort Niagara and because its irregular shape made it difficult to defend. By the time of Canadian Confederation in 1867, the few buildings that remained had rotted away and the site was turned over to grazing sheep and cattle.

Rebuilding Fort George fell to the Niagara Parks Commission, which purchased the land and recreated the military establishment during the 1930s. A national historic site, Fort George is now maintained by Parks Canada as a living history and one of Niagara's most prized attractions.

Fort George has been faithfully restored to its original condition, when it was the bulwark of British power and influence in the Niagara Region. It would have been in a state of disrepair when Sarah Ann lived and died there.

When visiting Fort George, it's not surprising to come across a ghost or two. After all, the fort housed soldiers who endured the horrors of war, and its battlements experienced the roar of musketry and cannons first-hand. It isn't unusual to hear stories of ethereal sentinels standing guard upon the parapets, disembodied drums rolling across the grounds, or phantom gunfire. The fort was reduced by artillery fire, so it isn't shocking when stories emerge of buildings that flicker in and out of existence.

Stepping through the ominous walls of Fort George to explore its shadowy history is a powerful experience, Upton explains. Darkness takes on a whole new meaning at Fort George after the sun sets. The ancient fortification becomes spectacularly eerie under lantern light, and soon you begin to imagine lurking monsters behind every corner or with every rustled leaf. "There are spectral horses, a door that appears at night but doesn't exist during the light of day, shadowy soldiers, and an ethereal cat — the fort is awash in spectral energy. We can't promise you'll have an otherworldly encounter, but with the fort so spiritually active, many people do," Upton says.

As Upton knows, it would take an entire book to chronicle all of the restless spirits lingering within the confines of Fort George. Instead, we've chosen to focus on a few spectral hot spots and one particularly beloved ghost.

SARAH ANN

Some might consider it odd to come across the spirit of a child in a military fortress that has been witness to so much bloodshed and violence, but it isn't, since higher ranking soldiers often brought their families with them to military postings. When guests tour the grounds of Fort George, they're frequently followed by a small presence looking for playmates to pass the time with. This young girl, named Sarah Ann, is certainly the most active and precocious spirit on the site.[6]

Over the years, Sarah Ann has been seen numerous times, and her youthful antics never fail to bring a smile to the faces of witnesses. Like a typical child, she's cheerful, mischievous, innocent, and eternally playful. She'll engage in games of peek-a-boo, hiding under beds and behind pillars, and giggling quietly to herself. Sometimes Sarah Ann will playfully tug on someone's clothes and then run away so that the victim of the prank only sees a momentary glimpse of a bare-footed girl with shoulder-length, curly blond hair wearing a flowing white dress before she disappears from view. On one tour, three women reported seeing a small, ethereal hand resting on a staircase railing. On another, a white cloud, vaguely human-oid in shape and child-sized was seen by a tourist. High-pitched giggling is frequently heard in the barracks, where Sarah Ann seems to spend most of her afterlife hours.

Ghost Tours of Niagara offers the opportunity to venture into the shad-ows of Fort George on many nights during the summer and into October. Sometimes people's lives are changed by what they encounter while on tour. Such was the case with two couples one night in August of 1995. At the end of the tour, the four individuals were walking along the road to return to their cars, approaching a pair of costumed guides. Skipping between the guides, so close it appeared as if the three were holding hands, was a little girl dressed in a white nightgown. She was the picture of inno-cence and cheerfulness. As the guides drew closer to the guests, the little girl slowly started to fade from view. The guides had been unaware of the spirit skipping between them, as had the two male tourists, who had seen nothing amiss. It was only the two women who witnessed the fleeting image of the ghost, but they excitedly pointed it out at exactly the same time and told eerily similar stories of what they had seen.

Another encounter with Sarah Ann occurred on a dark and stormy night. The evening was completely overcast, and the clouds looming over-head threatened a torrential downpour. Lightning flashed in the distance, and thunder rumbled across the sky like far-off cannon fire; it was the ideal backdrop for a ghost story.

Kyle Upton was enthused and ready for an evening of storytelling. Usually the tales he wove were those shared with him by others, but this night would be different. This night, he would gain a story of his own. He had no way of knowing, as he led his group into the subterranean tunnel located at the back of the fort, that he was drawing closer to a personal encounter with Sarah Ann. Kyle stood at the end of the tunnel, partially obscured by the shadows except where the light cast by his lantern made him visible. He waited there for all the members of the group to file into the dark, oppressive corridor.

"I could see out over the people's heads and I could make out the entrance of the tunnel, a dim rectangle of blue-grey illuminated by the light reflecting from the clouds outside," Kyle recalls in *Niagara's Ghosts 2*. "I could also see a small figure silhouetted in that rectangle of light. I could make out a little child, standing just outside the tunnel entrance, peering into the tunnel toward me."

The girl would play hide-and-seek, showing herself for a moment and then disappearing the next. When visible, she would hop and skip and look around to see if anyone was watching, as if putting on a show for the guests. For a while Kyle thought that perhaps the young girl was part of the tour, but after doing a quick head count and determining that all were present, the truth began to sink in. He realized she had to be the ghost of Sarah Ann — a spirit he had heard about numerous times in the past but wasn't entirely sure he believed in. Kyle found himself wondering who this young child was and why she was so curious about the tour. Was she looking for a friend to play with, or simply bored and looking for anything of interest to occupy her time?

Kyle tried his best to continue with the tour, but he was distracted by the scene playing out at the end of the tunnel. "I nearly choked on my narrative at what I saw," he writes. "Whenever the sky was lit up by lightning and the tunnel entrance illuminated with a flash of white, all I saw were the stone walls of the powder magazine outside, never the child that I could see in the gloom, but as soon as the lightning flash had faded, as the thunder rattled the loopholes of the Octagonal Blockhouse above us, there was the little kid in the gloom just below the entrance to the tunnel." The young child continued to watch the tour and waited patiently for the people to exit the tunnel. Then, as if suddenly tiring of their company, she was gone.

In 2014, Ian Russell and Trudy Shearing, co-founders of Ghost Hunt Paranormal, took part in one of Fort George's lantern-lit ghost tours. Like any good paranormal investigator, they brought EVP recorders with them and employed them whenever it was safe to do so without disrupting the remainder of the tour. At one point they were alone inside a building that houses jail cells and reasoned, "What better time to try the digital recorder?" Trudy asked if anyone would speak to them, but after several tense minutes without reply, the pair reluctantly left and rejoined the group.

The eerie tunnel at Fort George, where visitors often feel the cold chill of an unseen presence drifting past them.

Later, however, upon playing back the recording, they heard something that shocked them. Trudy's request for any present spirits to communicate with them was followed by three distinct words.

"Yes, I'm trying."

This remarkable piece of evidence spurred their interest in Fort George and its spectral garrison. They began negotiating for an opportunity to enter the park alone after dark in order to conduct an official paranormal investigation. Ian and Trudy were understandably thrilled when permission was eventually granted and a date in October 2016 was set. It would be just the two of them within the fort's walls, two lone figures enveloped by almost preternatural darkness and silence; their only company being whatever spirits chose to accompany them on their exploration of the grounds.

One of the spirits that joined that evening may well have been little Sarah Ann.

The sun had long since disappeared below the horizon, casting the world into deep shadow, when Ian and Trudy approached #2 Blockhouse. This imposing structure houses soldiers' barracks where an enlisted man and — if he was fortunate enough to have one — his family would have lived in meagre comfort. The investigators were on the main floor using their Spirit Box communication device when a tiny voice was heard.

"Story," it clearly said.

Ian and Trudy were ecstatic. A few moments later the same little voice said the same word: "Story." The spirit was insistent, because shortly thereafter it said "Story" for a third time.

The way the spirit repeated that same word over and over brings to mind the nagging of a small child desperately trying to wear their parents down in order to get their own way. That's certainly the conclusion Ian and Trudy came to.

"We made contact with who we believe to be the spirit of the little girl, Sarah Ann," Ian explains. "Now, that's very interesting, because on Kyle Upton's ghost tours, he says that Sarah Ann likes to sit on the stairs which go up to the second floor of the barracks and, from there, listen to the stories. We also know that Sarah Ann apparently enjoys following the Ghost Tours. I believe the voice was Sarah Ann, and she wanted us to tell her a story that night."

It's now well-established that a little soul lingers in Fort George. But just who is this child, and how did she come about haunting a place associated with soldiers and war? A tombstone in St. Mark's Cemetery may provide the answers. There, under the canopy of ageless trees, stands a tombstone to Sarah Ann Tracey, a child who was only seven years old when she died in 1840. She lived at Fort George with her mother, Hannah, and her father, Thomas, the troop sergeant major with the King's Dragoon Guards. Sadly, the manner of Sarah Ann's death and details of her life are unknown; the parish death records for 1840 have been lost, and there is no record of her parents in the parish marriage, baptismal, or death records.

Sarah Ann lies at rest in St. Mark's Cemetery, but little is known about her life and the nature of her death.

The similarities between the historical Sarah Ann and the spectral girl at Fort George are too eerie to ignore. Many people familiar with the story, Kyle Upton among them, have no doubt that these two children are one and the same. The search for her identity may well be over, but for Sarah Ann, her search continues for playmates, the parents she lost so long ago, and perhaps eventually eternal peace. For some reason she remains trapped within the walls of historic Fort George, a place where past and present, legend and history, live side by side, and every so often merge with alarming results.

OFFICERS' QUARTERS

Sitting at the centre of the fort and facing the gate on the other side of the parade ground, the Officers' Quarters is the most distinctive building within Fort George. Unlike the other buildings within the fort, which are either left with their square-strewn timbers exposed or painted a dull blue-grey that feels cold and dreary, this building is painted a warm and welcoming bright yellow. It also has more windows than other buildings, allowing sunlight to stream in, making rooms feel airy and alive. Fruit trees grow on the grounds alongside, and the entire compound is encircled by a welcoming, homey white picket fence. It's obvious to even the untrained eye that someone of importance resided there.

Indeed, wealthy, well-bred officers, like ensigns, lieutenants, and captains, would have resided here (more senior officers assigned to Fort George would have been able to afford their own homes in the nearby town). These junior officers were required to remain on base round-the-clock to oversee the training, discipline, and administration of the fort and its soldiers. After all, a senior officer couldn't be expected to leave the warmth of his bed in the middle of the night to ensure sentries were posted, or to wake in the pre-dawn gloom to oversee the daily roll call as soldiers gathered on the parade ground. That would be unseemly of a senior officer. Instead, these mundane tasks were left to the younger, less experienced officers.

These junior officers were privileged young men, and their accommodations were quite luxurious in keeping with the standards to which they were used to. Inside, instead of the spartan furnishings found in the enlisted men's barracks, you find plush feather beds, fine furniture, and luxuries the average soldier could only dream of. The best food and plenty of expensive alcohol would have been served, and cigar smoke would have hung heavily in the air. The atmosphere of the place would have been more akin to a gentleman's social club than a military post, with the officers spending much of their time playing the pianoforte, gambling and gaming, reading fine literature, and hosting parties where they danced with young ladies of the community under the watchful eyes of their escorts. Before war came to ruin things, a posting at Fort George was a plum one for young officers sent to serve in Canada.

It's been more than 150 years since British soldiers have lived in Fort George, and yet not all of them have given up residence. Cut down in battle with the balance of their lives still ahead of them, one or more young officers returned to the Officers' Quarters to haunt its luxurious rooms. Why lurk upon the forlorn battlefield where you fell when you can enjoy a far more cheerful atmosphere there? Why continue to lie in a rotting coffin when you can rest in comfort in a plush bed? Given the choice, the ghostly officers understandably made their way back to the last place they called home, the Officers' Quarters at Fort George.

Apparitions and bizarre phenomenon are frequently reported within the building. Voices whisper in ears, spectral hands shove the living, candles are blown out, and flashlights mysteriously die. Visitors report seeing an ethereal cat jumping off furniture to hide under a couch or table, or hear whispered conversation. Long dead officers are seen going about the routines of their previous lives. Sometimes these men are wispy figures, transparent and foggy, while at other times they seem like flesh and blood.

Many times over the years, staff and visitors have reported hearing the hauntingly beautiful sounds of the pianoforte playing by itself and witnessing keys moving as if by graceful invisible fingers. More than once staff members have even reported hearing the sound of a late-night party in progress within the Officers' Quarters. There's music and singing, the sounds of heels clicking on wood as women are twirled by suitors, and the hum of conversation — it's unmistakably a party in full swing. And yet, when the doors are unlocked and the building is entered, the partygoers melt away and the sounds disappear. Once, a costumed interpreter assigned to the Officers' Quarters for the day decided to play the pianoforte. She was a talented musician, so she occasionally took the opportunity to both entertain guests and indulge her passion. Halfway through her rendition, however, the woman felt a shiver run down her spine. Though it defied logic, the tune she was playing was not the song that was emerging. It was as if the pianoforte had a mind of its own, playing a song of its preference.

Another common phenomenon within the Officers' Quarters involves the canopy-draped bed within. Staff members entering in the morning often find the blanket and mattress indented with shape of a person in the middle of it, as if someone had been sleeping on it not long before. The perplexed staff member then tightens the springs, fluffs the bolster, turns over the mattress, and then tucks in and smooths the sheets and blankets. Its picture perfect, just as a nineteenth-century military man would have left it, and ready for the day's visitors. At the end of business hours, before locking up, the bed is checked again to ensure it remains perfectly made. By the following morning, the dent inevitably returns. "The sagging bed is a real mystery because it looks just like someone has been lying on top, although anyone doing so would have been detected by the alarm," says Ron Dale. "The only explanation that most come up with is that the ghost, a former British officer, has decided to rest his head on this bed, leaving his mark behind for staff to discover."

Kyle Upton admits that the ghosts within the Officers' Quarters appear to be unusually active during the Halloween season, when traditional folklore says spirits are more easily able to cross the barrier from the realm of the dead into the world of the living. The next two stories seem to add credence to Upton's observation.

The guided ghost tour of Halloween night in 1997 began innocently enough, but while the group passed through the Officers' Quarters, an elderly gentleman suddenly grew quite upset. His face drained of colour and he was visibly rattled. When asked what was wrong, he pointed a shaky finger toward a table in the sitting room. Trembling, he said he had seen two soldiers there, dressed in the distinctive red uniforms of the nineteenth century British army. One of these men sat in a chair, leaning intently over the table as he studied curled maps and assorted papers. He seemed absorbed in his work, occasionally taking notes with a feather quill. The other was a younger man who stood behind the other man's chair and peered over his shoulder at the documents. The elderly man had thought for a second that they were re-enactors, but realized his mistake when they faded from view. Were these officers still performing staff work or planning a campaign in a war that has been over for two hundred years?

The following Halloween was marked with another, equally powerful experience. That year, a relatively new member of the Ghost Tours of Niagara team was assigned security within the Officers' Quarters. It was his job to ensure that none of the precious artifacts within were stolen or broken, and to prevent the public from entering without their guides present. Though a new hire, the young man was level-headed, not given to flights of fancy, and completely nonplussed about the possible existence of ghosts, so the thought of spending a few hours alone in a haunted building didn't concern him. In truth, he had no idea what he was in store for.

There were long lulls between the arrival of the tours, which meant the young man was alone in the building for lonely stretches, with only a candle's flickering flame for company and lighting. During one such lull, the young man heard the sounds of footsteps shuffling through the halls. Thinking perhaps it was a straying member of one of the tour groups, he went to investigate. With only the slender flame of his candle, the employee made his way through the building, searching the shadows and calling out to whomever may have ventured into the building. Though several times the footsteps sounded nearby, as if coming from the next room, he never saw anyone. That left only one explanation: the culprit was one of the ghosts said to inhabit the building. This realization caused his heart to race and the skin on his arms was covered with goose bumps.

With nothing to be done about a ghostly intruder, the young man went back to his original post to await the arrival of the upcoming tour group. He continued to hear shuffling footsteps through the halls, but willed himself to pay no attention to them. But he couldn't ignore what happened next. Suddenly, and despite the absence of any sort of wind, the man's candle blew out, casting him into fear-inducing pitch darkness. Stumbling for matches with shaky fingers, the young man had no sooner got the candle lit again when it mysteriously blew out once more. He struck another, and in the quivering flame thought he caught momentary sight of a shadowy figure in the room with him. His throat was suddenly dry, as fear began to take hold.

Then the doors within the building started to open and close on their own. Finally, after what seemed like hours of torture but was likely only a few minutes, the young man's courage finally failed him and he ran outside. He refused to re-enter, demanding a new assignment somewhere — anywhere — else. It was clear to him that, for some reason he couldn't fathom, he wasn't welcome in the Officers' Quarters.

Sonja is a long-time employee of Fort George who refuses to step so much as a foot into the Officers' Quarters after dark, fearful of what lurks within the building's darkness. Her wariness is the result of the terrifying events of a night that she can never forget.

When Fort George closed its doors to the tourist crowd at the end of that particular day, it was Sonja's task to lock up the Officers' Quarters and set its alarm. Before she could do so, she had to sweep through the building to ensure no one was being locked inside. While she was passing through the building, Sonja had an unsettling feeling that there was someone in the building with her, intently watching her. It gnawed at her, but she found no one, and concluded that it was merely her imagination. Only a few hours later, Sonja returned to the fort to open up for the night's ghost tour. She found the Officers' Quarters exactly as she had left it earlier. Lighting the candle, she noted the same uncomfortable atmosphere within. She didn't linger long, locking the building up tight again and putting the sense of creeping malice behind her.

Later that evening, the ghost tour approached the Officers' Quarters, its members unaware of the unsettling feeling that had chased Sonja away. The tour guide urged his excited followers to huddle around the window looking into the sitting room while he began to relate some of the many paranormal events that people have witnessed in the building over the years. As the guide was talking, a number of guests who were peering through the window jumped back in horror. They had seen the door within swing swung shut on its own. When they excitedly related what they'd seen to the tour guide, he could offer no explanation.

This was the final straw for Sonja. She knew the door was heavy and its hinges stiff, requiring considerable effort to push it closed. A breeze, even if there had been one sweeping into the building, could not have been responsible. She was holding the only keys accessing the building, so no one could have entered and closed the door to startle the guests. There was no earthly explanation. Sonja couldn't explain how the door could have closed, which only added to the unease that had settled over her all day long while in the building. When she had to blow out the candle at the end of the tours for that night, she did so hurriedly. She then locked the door, set the alarm, and quickly made her way to the front gates. To her horror, as she was racing across the grounds, Sonja heard the distinct sound of the antique pianoforte playing from within the locked and alarmed Officers' Quarters.

The night's events were so traumatic that she promised to never again lock up the Officers' Quarters by herself, a promise that she faithfully kept.

While most of the young and ambitious men who once resided within the Officers' Quarters at Fort George have peacefully made the transition to the other side, the spirits of several remain behind, lost and confused. Cut down in battle, for them the War of 1812 has never ended. They are the greatest victims of the war, as even in death they've been unable to find the peace that had been promised to them by army chaplains.

Why do these spirits occasionally act out? Maybe it is regret and anger that they died before their lives had really truly begun, and that all they got for their service to King and Country was a headstone in a distant corner of the Empire. Or perhaps it is out of indignation that their quarters, a place once reserved only for well-born gentlemen, is being intruded upon by tourists ... commoners! In either case, those who enter the Officers' Quarters after dark had best steel themselves for the worst, as something is undoubtedly lurking in the darkness, just beyond the lantern light.

FORMER GIFT SHOP

One of the most haunted locations within Fort George is also perhaps the most unlikely: a modest frame structure that doesn't appear martial in any way. Until very recently, this unassuming building housed the fort's gift shop, and today serves as a staff kitchen. During its time as a gift shop, it was a cheerful building, where happy tourists explored shelves full of books and mementoes of a fun-filled day exploring Canada's military past. But what these tourists didn't know, what park staff rarely discussed with the public, was that the gift shop had a long tradition of unexplained paranormal activity. As a result, it came as quite a shock when a whispered voice was heard, an item suddenly flew off a shelf, or when stepping into a cold spot so chilled it caused goose bumps to crawl over flesh, even on a hot summer's day.

Such chilling phenomenon occurred too often to be the figment of an overactive imagination or to simply wave away as one might when strangeness interrupts the safe structure of our lives. These episodes were the creeping tendrils of a troubled past reaching into the present, hinting at despair and torment that stained the very ground the building was built on.

To understand this paranormal mar, we need to take a step back in time to explore their origins. While the building is modern-built, it sat on the location of the former garrison hospital, built in 1799 while Fort George was still in its infancy. Stories circulate today that mortally wounded or terminally ill soldiers were sent to the building's basement to die so they were not occupying valuable bed space or unnerving other patients with their last cries of suffering. This is nothing more than an urban legend, a colourful myth that helps make for a great story. Nevertheless, the hospital was a grim place.

The War of 1812 saw the post surgeon overworked with gruesome battlefield injuries. Dozens of wounded soldiers, their limbs shattered by cannonballs or with musket balls buried deep in their flesh, were pulled from the battlefield of Queenston Heights and raced to the hospital at Fort George. The hospital would have been utter chaos after battle, with blood streaming onto the floorboards until they were covered with crimson pools and slippery underfoot, bloodied rags and uniforms tossed about, and the screams of the wounded and dying a maddening cacophony. It would have been a nightmare straight out of hell, a place of misery and suffering. Many of the men would inevitably die of their wounds, despite the surgeon's best efforts.

The blood and suffering of these traumatic events stained the ground upon which the hospital stood and are said to have sparked the hauntings that afflicted the current building when it was built in 1940. Originally, and for decades after being built, the wood-frame structure served as the residence of successive Fort George caretakers. It was during this period, the story goes, that the spirit or spirits first began to make their presence felt. Although the first grounds manager and his family lived in the fort for many years without incident, the same cannot be said of his replacement. Items that disappeared and reappeared at random, as well as unusual noises and strange lights that plagued the family at all hours had them on the verge of nervous collapse. They had no choice but to leave after only two years, driven out by spirits that, for some unknown reason, resented their presence.

The strange events continued even after the home was transformed into a gift shop. Many tourists left the building bewildered and unnerved by a variety of paranormal activity. A few years ago, for example, a female visitor went to use the bathroom located in the building. While there, she was startled to hear the distinct sound of footsteps treading directly overhead, despite the fact that the building had no second floor. She fled from the building and shared her experience with her husband, who was waiting patiently outside. He was naturally dubious but also somewhat curious, so convinced her to go back into the bathroom. Sure enough, after entering the facilities they both distinctly heard the sound of heavy footsteps pacing back and forth on the floor above: *thump, thump, thump.*

Thinking they were the butt of a practical joke, the two of them ran outside and circled the building, hoping to catch the prankster in the act or find any explanation for the noises they both heard. But even after circling the building several times they found no one and nothing that could possibly explain the footsteps. There was no sign of a person, or an animal for that matter, who might have been responsible. The couple was reluctantly forced to conclude that the sounds were not made by the living.

A possible explanation emerges if one digs a bit into the history of the building. A painting of the fort made by a military surgeon stationed in Niagara-on-the-Lake just before the War of 1812 depicts the hospital building as having a second floor. Could it be that an entity from long ago haunts the upper floor, trudging across floorboards that haven't existed for two hundred years?

Fort George plays host to lantern-lit ghost tours throughout the operating season. During one such ghost tour in the summer of 2002, Wendy happened to look up toward the gift shop. Near the back of the building on the side wall, she saw a rectangular doorway blazing with orange light. It almost looked as though the building was on fire, so the woman breathed a sigh of relief when the light faded moments later. At least the building wasn't about to burn down before her eyes. But fear was soon replaced by disbelief. What had caused the light? One of the security guards on duty that night had witnessed the unusual glow as well and had no explanation. The gift shop was closed for the evening and locked up tight, so no one could have been inside to turn on a light. It was a mystery.

In August 1996, a new guide followed along on one of the ghost tours for training purposes. As he walked alongside the crowd, he looked in the direction of the gift shop and was bewildered to see an almost transparent man standing just behind the building. In the evening gloom it took a few moments for his vision to focus, and as it did, he was horrified. He noticed that the apparition was wearing a bloodstained white smock. As the young guide inched closer to the building, he could see that the luminous figure was also carrying a bucket of what seemed like severed human limbs. The figure then disappeared in the blink of an eye.

Later that year, more and more reports came in from tour participants who reported sightings of the same man, dressed in white and standing near the gift shop. No one really knows who this spirit is, but those who have witnessed the apparition believe that he was a surgeon of long ago, perhaps a man to whom fell the grim task of amputating shattered limbs in the aftermath of the Battle of Queenston Heights.

The basement storeroom seems to be a focus of spectral activity. Lights are known to turn on and off in the basement as if a ghostly hand were playing with the switch. Similarly, the motion activated lights in the new bathroom flare to life at night despite the fact that the building is empty and locked. In addition, mysterious figures are sometimes seen through windows moving around inside the building at all hours. When staff race to confront the intruder, they inevitably find no one, as if the figure had simply faded away into nothingness.

The ghosts of Fort George's former hospital died in situations that evoked extreme emotion, so it is little wonder that one or more were not able to find peace even as their mortal bodies mouldered in their graves. The continued suffering of these ghosts, trapped in a purgatory between the realms of the living and the dead, is a reminder of the true tragedy of war.

15

ST. MARK'S CEMETERY

Ghosts from the past roam the streets on equal footing with the tourists in Niagara-on-the-Lake. And nowhere do they seem closer than in the cemetery behind St. Mark's Anglican Church, where ancient tombstones corroded by time stand under stately old trees.

It's said that Major General Isaac Brock, commander-in-chief of the British forces in Upper Canada during the War of 1812, used to sit on a rock in the middle of this burial ground, plotting battles and keeping an eye on the enemy just across the Niagara River. The fabled rock is still there, and while Brock no longer is, the spirits of many of his beloved soldiers may well be.[1]

The cemetery at St. Mark's is one of the oldest in Ontario. Even before the cemetery was established in 1792 to serve the village of Newark (as Niagara-on-the-Lake was then called) and the surrounding area, the grounds had been used for centuries as a First Nations burial site. Dozens, perhaps hundreds, of First Nations people were laid to rest there, and then disturbed when the area was dug up to bury European settlers.[2]

The earliest headstone dates back to 1794, but because Newark was a small community, only a handful of others joined it over the next two decades.[3] That all changed in the autumn of 1812, when the United States declared war on Britain and invaded her North American colonies. For the next four years, the Niagara Frontier became a hotly contested battleground. Hundreds fell on each side, with many of those who fought under the British banner ending up at St. Mark's Cemetery.

In fact, St. Mark's has literally been scarred by that conflict of long ago. The church was pressed into service as a hospital to treat the soldiers gruesomely wounded in battle.[4] Among the most common wounds were limbs shattered by bullets and infected with gangrene. Surgeons had no recourse but to amputate if lives were to be saved. Deep gouges left by the surgeon's axe can still be seen in several flat tombstones that served as impromptu operating beds.[5]

Running your fingers over the jagged scars, you can easily imagine the horror of those moments. The victim is in agony, his heart pounding at the sight of the axe and its implication. He might accept that losing a limb is a small price to pay for saving his life, but the thought of further pain is too much for him to bear. He thrashes about wildly, and it takes the combined efforts of four of his comrades to hold him still. His eyes bulge in terror as the axe is brought over the surgeon's head. The blade falls, cutting through skin, flesh, and bone. It's too much to bear, so the victim passes out. Blood splatters all over the surgeon, but he's performed

Evidence of brutality? Many believe these marks in the headstones were made during hasty battlefield amputations.

so many amputations over the last few days that he barely notices anymore. He wipes the red from his face and grimly moves on to the next patient. The limb is thrown to the side, another addition to an ever-growing pile of discarded arms and legs.

Undoubtedly, many of these soldiers never recovered from the primitive surgery, dying either from blood loss or infection. They would have been buried at the cemetery, perhaps only a few feet from where the amputations occurred. If you give your imagination free rein, you can sense the presence of these soldiers. Some people actually see or hear them.

The list of supernatural phenomena associated with the cemetery is lengthy and frightening. Many have seen ghostly soldiers, oftentimes missing an arm or fading away at the hip; evidence, perhaps, that the men died after having a limb amputated. Others have seen ghost lights dancing around the tombstones, casting an eerie glow in an already macabre setting. Many witnesses have reported hearing disembodied, ear-piercing screams of sheer agony or the commands of officers who have long since died. Some have detected a sickening, rotting smell like that which can only come from a decomposing corpse. There are even reports of spectral First Nations people lurking amidst the shadows — spirits who have undoubtedly been disturbed by the burials that desecrated their sacred grounds.

Psychics, or people sensitive to the rhythms of the other side, have had even more troubling experiences among the leaning headstones of St. Mark's. While exploring the site, Pauline Raby, a psychic who assisted paranormal researcher John Savoie in compiling the book *Shadows of Niagara*, reported feeling pain in her limbs that reflected amputations. She sensed many ghosts lingering in the cemetery, victims of a long-ago war who continue to suffer from their ghastly wounds.[6]

These men-at-arms have served their country for nearly two centuries now — a ghostly company defending Niagara-on-the-Lake from a non-existent foe. Unfortunately, at least one account suggests they may have become disillusioned and embittered with their eternal obligation to King and Country.

A man happened to be making his way past the church one night when he saw a strange glow emerging from the lifeless depths of the cemetery. Intrigued, perhaps even entranced, he crept forward for a closer look. He saw a dark-haired man in what appeared to be an old-fashioned military uniform staring down at a spot on the ground. He held a lit candle in one hand, and it was this candle that cast the ghostly illumination. He looked sad, the candle's glow accentuating his tormented features. A shiver ran down the witness's spine. With a sense of horror, he realized that the ghost was looking for what was no longer there: one of his arms!

As if he had suddenly become aware he was no longer alone, the ghost looked up and his hollow eyes met those of his trembling audience. Their eyes locked. The man was terrified by what he saw. Looking back at him was a face with bone-white skin stretched tight over protruding bones, and he suddenly felt a chill colder than death shudder through his body. He sensed within the ghost a jealous longing for a lifelong past.

To the man's relief, after only a few moments the ghostly image began to fade. That wasn't the last of the unsettling encounter, however. Far from it. "I think I brought the ghost home with me that night because weird, unexplainable things began happening in my house ... things that had never happened before," says the man, who prefers that his name not appear in print.

It began with a general sense of unease, as if someone was watching him all the time. Occasionally, there would even be momentary touches, as if someone was brushing against him. Several times he awoke, convinced that someone was standing over his bed, looming over him with sinister intent. Each time, his eyes would adjust to the dark and he'd find himself alone. Yet the feeling persisted.

"There were two occasions when I returned home to find a deadbolt across the door that could only be locked from the inside. There was nobody there, and as far as I knew, nobody had been there. I had to crawl through a window both times.... I removed the deadbolt after the second incident."

It seemed as if the ghost was trying to keep the man out of his own home, though the reason why remains a mystery. Also a mystery is what drove the ghost away, for shortly after the deadbolt was removed, the oppressive atmosphere in the home was suddenly lifted. The man hasn't experienced any unusual activity since, for which he is thankful.

"Needless to say, I haven't gone past St. Mark's after dark since then."[7]

Another encounter occurred more recently, and in broad daylight, when a pair of ghost enthusiasts, Jennifer and Matt, decided to tour the grounds. As soon as they stepped foot on hallowed ground, both noticed a sudden chill in the air, though neither could tell if it was the anticipation of walking into one of the most haunted cemeteries in Ontario or simply dampness from the light mist that fell upon them. It was as if the day was set for ghost-hunting: a sombre, grey, cloudy sky above, haziness all around, and fall colours dancing in the wind. If St. Mark's did have any spirits hanging around, it would be on a day like this that they just might make their presence known.

It didn't take long to locate the tombstones upon which the soldiers had underwent amputation two centuries ago, and both visitors were moved by the implication of the gashes clearly visible in the aged stone. Being near a place where so much pain and sorrow had occurred caused Jennifer to shudder inwardly. She felt something pull her to one particular tombstone, and before she knew it her hands were caressing the smooth stone. It was cold against her warm fingers, almost painful, like touching a block of ice.

Suddenly, a lonely soldier's agonizing cries called out to her. An image began to play out before her eyes like a grainy film.

A young soldier, no more than twenty, lay upon the tombstone before her. Looming over him was a doctor, his uniform stained crimson and his hands covered in gore. Beside the surgeon stood three silently praying nuns, rosaries pressed between white-knuckled fingers. The soldier's legs were shattered below the knees. Nothing remained of them except for a mass of mangled flesh, splintered bone, and blood-soaked woolen pants. He was so scared and shaking uncontrollably. Even though agony clouded his senses, he knew what was about to happen.

A mixture of sympathy and determination was etched on the doctor's face. He was clearly filled with sorrow, but understood the necessity of what he was about to do. Towering over his screaming patient, he raised a blood-ied axe above his head and allowed it to fall down on the young soldier's leg. The sound of axe head biting through flesh and bone horrified Jennifer. It's a sound she'll never forget.

The pain was unbearable. So much so that just as the doctor raised the axe to take the other shattered limb, the young soldier passed out. The whole time, the holy sisters prayed for the patient, and waited to carry him into the church where they hoped he would recover from his terrible wounds.

The stories of ghosts floating among the aging stones in the cemetery at St. Mark's are well known. There are those who believe the church is also haunted by a former priest.

For a moment Jennifer almost forgot where she was. She had been so engrossed in the drama unfolding before her eyes that she had lost track of place and time. But even after she returned to the twenty-first century and the guns of the War of 1812 were two centuries behind her, she couldn't escape the lasting effects of the terrible scene she had witnessed. In fact, she felt the presence of the young soldier, now a ghost trapped in a world foreign to him, standing nearby. Clearly he had never recovered from the amputation, one among many soldiers who gave their lives for our country and now lie at rest in St. Mark's Cemetery.[8]

Despite its troubled history, St. Mark's Anglican Church and Cemetery bears its wounds and sorrows like badges of honour. Well-maintained, the cemetery is a reminder of a painful era in Canadian history. Though faded, the headstones from the War of 1812 look sturdy enough to stand for another two hundred years. And as long as they do stand, the ghostly soldiers will continue to roam amongst them, searching for lost limbs and lost lives.

16
SHORT TAKES FROM BEYOND THE GRAVE

While researching this book, we uncovered dozens of locations across Niagara-on-the-Lake said to be disturbed by ghostly presences and other paranormal activity. It proved impossible to provide a comprehensive overview of the community's hauntings in one book; to do so would have meant sacrificing the depth of research and richness of storytelling, which we believe makes this book unique and appealing.

In capsule form, here are some of the chilling tales that didn't make the cut.

HAWLEY-BRECKENRIDGE HOUSE

This magnificent home, built in 1796, is among the oldest in Niagara-on-the-Lake, surviving the razing of the community by American forces in 1813. (It was torched and partially burned, but the flames miraculously did not complete the destruction.) In 1876, Queen Victoria's son, Edward, the Prince of Wales, spent a night or two in the home during a tour of Niagara. Perhaps the noted philanderer shared a room with Elizabeth, the young woman in a flowing grey gown whose spirit haunts the building.

Little is known of Elizabeth. It is said that she died in the Hawley-Breckenridge House in the mid-nineteenth century and loved her earthly residence so much that she refuses to be evicted from her home, even in death. One reliable witness, a very serious British army officer, was reported to have seen the apparition of a beautiful woman who appeared and disappeared like wisps of smoke. She is most frequently encountered in the upstairs bedrooms and hallways, but has been seen several times standing on the front steps, looking out onto a world she no longer recognizes.

It's believed she may be kept company by the spirit of escaped slaves. For a time, the Hawley-Breckenridge House was used as a safe house for runaway slaves escaping the oppression of the United States. Some completed the harrowing journey successfully, only to die without enjoying the freedom they were willing to risk their lives for. Six of these unfortunate individuals were buried in the backyard of the home, but local legends suggest they do not rest easy in their graves.

OBAN INN

Captain Duncan Mallory, a man who would earn his fortune by establishing the first steamship service between Toronto and Niagara, built this home around 1824. It became a fine hotel in 1895, and served in that capacity for a century until a devastating fire in 1992 chased guests from their Christmas dinner and almost completely destroyed the building. The Oban Inn was painstakingly and accurately reconstructed, and was reopened a year later.

The fire did nothing to chase away the two guests who, despite the passage of decades, refuse to check out of their accommodations. One is Captain Mallory himself, a man as dignified in death as he was in life, appearing before startled guests as if to welcome them into his home but refusing to partake in childish antics. The other spirit is an old woman who wears a cook's uniform, and may have been an employee at the inn during the early twentieth century.

CHARLES INN

The Charles Inn, today a small hotel, was built by local lawyer Charles Richardson immediately upon his nomination to Parliament in 1832 (he served on behalf of Niagara until 1834). Overnight guests share the premises with several noisy ghosts. During an otherwise enjoyable stay in the charming hotel, a couple was kept up all night by two women talking and giggling in the adjoining room. Come morning, they decided to complain to management, only to discover they were the only guests checked in.

Unusual noises are occasionally heard from the basement as well, and a shadowy man has been seen there at least once. Could this ghost have anything to do with the long-vaulted chamber in the cellar, which local lore says is a secret tunnel to Fort Mississauga?

MOFFAT INN

The Moffat Inn has enjoyed the title of longest-serving hotel in Niagara-on-the-Lake — for over 180 years! It was built in 1835 by William Moffat, a career hotelier who previously owned and operated the Sign of the Crown Inn (today called the Stocking House, located at 118 Johnson Street), and from the very beginning served as a tavern and hotel.

The ghostly activity in the Moffat Inn is largely confined to a single room, where people have reported seeing odd lights, sometimes described as orb-like, other times like the flickering flame of a candle. Strange, inexplicable noises come from this room; when people investigate their source, they find nothing. And several times people have witnessed picture frames shifting on their own, as if being manipulated by unseen hands.

BUTLER'S BARRACKS

Butler's Barracks is a testament to the lengthy military presence at Niagara-on-the-Lake. The first buildings erected on the site were built in 1796 to serve the Indian Department, a British military organization whose role was to maintain ties with First Nations Peoples in both Canada and what is now the United States. The buildings were destroyed during the War of 1812, but they were later rebuilt and became home to a substantial military presence after the war. For more than a century, thousands of soldiers were trained there for overseas duty in the Boer War, both World Wars, and the Korean War. Today, it is a museum for the Welland and Lincoln Regiment.

With such a long and diverse history, it's probably natural that the site is haunted by a disparate collection of ghosts. There are the British soldiers, dressed in their unmistakable red coats, seen marching past (and, in one case, through startled visitors). Then there are the two warriors, who seem so real that people believe them to be re-enactors. In every case, the witnesses claim to hear the grim-faced men conversing in their ancestral tongue. Finally, there are the tragic Polish soldiers, sent here for training during the First World War, who were struck down by a flu epidemic in 1918 and buried far from home. They wander the grounds aimlessly, searching desperately for a means to return to their country.

177 KING STREET

A strange energy clings to this majestic Victorian home, and it's believed that a woman's spirit wanders within, desperately trying to pass on from this world to her eternal rest and a measure of peace. The hauntings began in earnest a few decades ago when the building was renovated for use as an art gallery. They didn't know that restoring the building would stir up something paranormal.

In the mid-1990s, a 911 operator working the late shift received a call from that house. She asks, "What's your emergency?" The only response is dead air — perhaps quiet literally, in this case. She asks a couple of more times, increasingly desperate with each attempt to encourage a response, but still nothing. It's deathly silent on the other end — no voice, no breathing, no background noise. Fearing the worst, the operator dispatches an ambulance. Arriving in a blaze of sirens and flashing red lights, the panicked EMTs find the building empty and no sign that a call had been made from it.

The incident was a bit strange, perhaps, but nothing particularly alarming. Until it happens again the next night: the same time, the same call, the same dead air, and the same two responding medics. This was a bit more concerning. By the time it happened for the fifth night in a row, the medics and the 911 operator were frightened and on-edge. Whoever was making these emergency calls was beyond any help.

And then, just as suddenly as the calls began, they ended.

In recent years, people participating in the haunted tours have reported all sorts of strange phenomenon — usually involving electronic devices — when the group pauses before the building to hear the story of the phantom 911 calls. Batteries on cameras and cellphones will mysteriously drain, shutting them off. As soon as they walk away from the home, the devices suddenly turn themselves back on. One man took a single picture, and it appeared an unlucky thirteen times in his gallery. Another individual took a picture only to find his entire gallery suddenly erased. Tour owner Daniel Cumerlato watched a man line up the entire house with his DSLR camera. He took the photo and it came back zoomed in on the stained glass window of the tower, even though he hadn't touched the manual zoom lens.

Perhaps the turbulent energy given off by the troubled spirit's nighttime wanderings inadvertently affects electronics? Or maybe she is attempting to communicate, to plead for help as she did those five nights in the 1990s?

We don't know who lingers in this beautiful home, but one hopes she transitions to the other side soon so her suffering might come to an end.

SILKS COUNTRY KITCHEN

Not every haunted location in Niagara-on-the-Lake has to be deeply steeped in history. By way of example, look no further than Silks Country Kitchen, a pleasant restaurant located in an innocuous modern building with no heritage to speak of. And yet, staff and diners alike believe the restaurant to be thoroughly haunted.

One time, a little girl of about six innocently asked one of the servers who a man sitting at a nearby window table was. Problem was, there was no one there. Security cameras have caught the back door swinging open by itself and a picture frame flying off a shelf, as if someone had thrown it in anger.

"I myself have witnessed numerous things at the restaurant," explains Cori Pecchia, who recently left Silks Country Kitchen after spending six years there as a server. "One time I went into the walk-in fridge and as I opened the freezer door, a head of frozen cabbage levitated off the top shelf, then flew through the air and hit me right in the middle of my forehead. Another time a customer was telling one of my fellow waitresses that she sensed a presence in the restaurant. Just as this was happening, I ran out of kitchen to tell my co-worker that a strainer had levitated into the air and dropped onto the deep freezer."

Once, Cori made the mistake of treating something lightly that should have been treated with respect. She thought it would be good fun to turn off the lights and ask the ghost to reveal itself in some manner. No sooner was the restaurant dark and the request to give a sign uttered, a wet floor sign inexplicably fell over. It was as if the ghost had said, in no uncertain terms, "There's your sign!"

Other staff have seen, or been the brunt of, eerie paranormal activity as well. A dishwasher had buckets thrown at him from across the room, thankfully without injury. Another waitress witnessed cutlery sliding off a table. The list of experiences from startled staff goes on and on. Suffice to say, several waitresses are wary of closing the restaurant.

No one knows who the ghost that haunts Silks Country Kitchen might be. Is he somehow connected to the owners, or, perhaps, is his attachment to the land itself? Maybe the ghostly man is simply a wandering spirit that has taken up residence here. More perplexing is why this spirit seems so agitated, and what is behind his angry outbursts of poltergeist activity.

ROYAL GEORGE THEATRE

The centrepiece of the Shaw Festival, the Royal George Theatre was built in 1915 as a vaudeville house known as the Lord Kitchener (after Field Marshal Horatio Kitchener, 1st Earl Kitchener, who served as Britain's secretary of state for war from 1914 to 1916) to entertain the tens of thousands of troops training at Fort Niagara during the First World War. After the war ended and the soldiers were gone, the theatre continued to host travelling roadshows for the entertainment of locals. In 1940 it was refurbished as a movie theatre and renamed the Brock Cinema. The theatre was renamed the Royal George Theatre in 1973, and when purchased by the Shaw Festival Foundation in 1980, it was refurbished to reflect the glory of a true Edwardian opera house.

The theatre is said to be haunted by a number of ghosts, including a prominent pair that were proud members of the Shaw Festival — one on stage, the other off. The first spirit is said to be that of Jeffrey Dallas, a former head of lighting design, who died in 1989. When the house lights are dimmed, theatre-goers swear they have seen the apparition of Dallas, still performing his duties even two decades after his death. Dallas takes dedication to one's job to unnatural lengths.

The second spirit is that of Nancy Kerr, an actress who spent a lot of time on the Shaw Festival stage before her death in 1991. Since then, a number of festival actors have seen her ethereal form throughout the building. They also claim her spirit makes her presence known on the stage during productions, occasionally bumping into actors while they perform their shows.

And, of course, there are believed to be many others as well, some dating back a century. Psychics who enter the building claim the Royal George has a pulse of its own. You can take the audiences and the performers and the stage crew out and it still lives on.

LIZZIE IN THE HAUNTED SHOP

Ghost Walks leads eager tourists through the darkened and hushed streets of Niagara-on-the-Lake, weaving chilling tales that provide an introduction to many of the restless wraiths that inhabit this historic community. With the moon poking through the clouds above to cast an eerie pale glow on the sleeping town, and a chilled wind moaning ominously, you soon find yourself imagining every shadow hides a lurking spirit and every rustling of leaves suggests the movement of some unseen ghoul. In short, it's a thrilling evening.

"Niagara-on-the-Lake is one of Canada's most haunted towns, with two hundred years of history and ghosts tied into its forts, inns, and homes. Our guides will make sure you 'meet' some of the many ghosts that inhabit this town," says Daniel Cumerlato, owner of Ghost Walks.

It's probably only appropriate that the Haunted Shop, the building from which the tours originate, should be graced with a paranormal presence as well.

"Lizzie is our resident haunted doll," explains Daniel. "She's sat in a small rocking chair in the window staring at customers going in and out of the shop since we moved to this location in 2012. But she doesn't always stay put…."

The following is just one example of the strangeness surrounding this eerie little doll.

A few years ago, an employee named Cathy was opening the shop. She saw Lizzie face-up on the floor in the middle of the shop. Cathy rationalized what she found by concluding that the doll must have fallen and rolled across the floor — even though that was highly unlikely, as the doll had come to rest some five feet from her window-side seat. Cathy went to retrieve the doll, and expected to find her delicate porcelain head smashed, but to her amazement Lizzie was completely undamaged. She put the doll back in her chair and tried to forget about the experience.

Ghost Walks leads participants through Niagara-on-the-Lake, sharing eerie tales from numerous spectrally active locations. It's perhaps appropriate that the Ghost Walks' gift shop, the Haunted Shop, has wraiths of its own — connected to the unsettled doll known as Lizzie.

The next day, however, Lizzie was once again on the floor, face-up and in the exact same spot as the day before.

Now frightened, Cathy was resolved not to have another similar experience, so she tied a string around Lizzie's neck, attaching her to the chair. The doll stayed there, but then Cathy had a string of misfortune that she described as the worst luck in her life. Nothing seemed to go right and she blamed the doll. Frustrated with her string of accidents and mishaps, Cathy personally removed the string and her life instantly reverted back to normal.

"The oddest part of the episode is Lizzie's porcelain head," explains Daniel. "Even if the doll was pushed by ghostly hands, the head would have smashed. She must have been carried and gently placed on the floor."

Or maybe, just maybe, she moved there by herself....

FORT GEORGE GUARDHOUSE

Fort George houses a veritable army of ghosts, but one is unique. It's not the apparition of a human being or even an animal. Instead, it's a true haunted house, a spectral building that somehow emerges from the past to intrude upon the twenty-first century.

The building in question is the fort's guardhouse. This building was important to any military base; it was here that sentries stood duty, restricting entrance to the grounds and ensuring security within. Within the guardhouse there would also have been a jail where soldiers under arrest for various transgressions — from relatively minor infractions, such as drunkenness, to serious crimes, like cowardice or disobeying orders — were locked up. Just outside the jail would be the flogging post, where offending soldiers were punished by being whipped with the cat o' nine tails.

During a 1997 ghost tour, a man and his two daughters heard the sound of scurrying feet in the gathering gloom from across the parade ground. They looked in that direction, eyes struggling to pierce the dusk, and saw an orange glow in one of the guardroom's windows. It was strangely unnerving, and then it faded. They reported what they had seen to the guide, and she was stunned by what they described: a rectangular window, higher than it was wide, quite unlike the small, square windows in the current reconstruction. The guide knew something that the general public would not; in the rush to get the fort built in the 1930s, the wrong blueprints were used for the guardhouse, so the building that stands today is very different than that from two hundred years ago. It seems as if the family had seen the guardhouse as it would have appeared two centuries ago.

This was no isolated incident. Several times the guardhouse of the past has revealed itself in the present. The appearance of the building is hard to explain and impossible to forget.

FORT GEORGE BASTION

Fort George has enough ghost stories to fill an entire book. One of the more tragic stories centres around a soldier assigned the task of standing sentry one frigid winter night in 1811. Collar pulled high in a desperate attempt to ward off the cold, he dutifully stood atop the bastion as a biting wind whipped off Lake Ontario. It wasn't long before the cold had gnawed its way through the soldier's clothes and began to numb his body. Perhaps without even realizing what was happening, the soldier slipped into a deep, hypothermia-induced sleep. He never awoke. It wasn't until the next morning that his frozen corpse, dusted with newly fallen snow, was discovered by the soldier sent to relieve him.

This tragic ghost remains vigilantly watching over Fort George to this day, unaware that the enemy he was assigned to watch against no longer exists. He walks back and forth on the bastion, musket shouldered, with only the glowing embers of his pipe to warm him. Oftentimes, only his upper torso is present, his legs disappearing into the parapet. Interestingly, this detail adds authenticity to sightings, since few would know that the bastion actually stands about three feet higher than it did in 1811. Sometimes, only the soldier's tall shako hat is visible as the undead Red Coat continues to guard the fort with unnatural vigilance.

"This ghost has been pretty quiet for some time," explains Kyle Upton. "There haven't been sightings in a while, but we're not sure why." Perhaps this soldier has finally been relieved of his duty and found some peace.

CHRISTIAN WARNER CEMETERY

Do the dead at this old cemetery emerge from their graves of their own free will, perhaps motivated by unfinished business in the mortal realm, or were they awoken from their eternal slumber by the recent construction on the adjacent Queen Elizabeth Way? No one knows for certain, but we do know that passing motorists have claimed to see eerie lights and shadowy figures moving about the weathered and leaning headstones late at night.

It's best to keep driving, however, because the ghosts don't like intruders. An investigating group of ghost hunters were chased from the cemetery when their flashlights all failed at the same time and a fierce voice emerging from the gloom ordered them to "Get out!" One woman even claims to have been bruised by a spectral slap across the face. Wisely, the ghost hunters never returned.

17
EXPERIENCE FOR YOURSELF

While we hope audiences find our book entertaining and informative, the best way to enjoy history and haunts is to experience it for yourself. Words on a page cannot replace the thrill of exploring a place in person. That reality was an important factor that determined which of Niagara-on-the-Lake's countless ghost stories would find a home in this book. We wanted readers to be able to visit the sites for themselves, so every paranormal location described herein is open to the public in one form or another.

LAURA SECORD HOMESTEAD
Travel back in time at Laura Secord's lovingly restored homestead. Restored and furnished with original furniture by the Laura Secord Candy Company in 1971, the home was then gifted to the Niagara Parks Commission in 1998. Guided tours led by costumed staff provide information about this heritage house, the hero who lived here, and the history of the area.

Location: 29 Queenston Street, Queenston
Phone: 905-262-4851
Email: info@niagaraparks.com
Website: www.niagaraparks.com/visit/heritage/laura-secord-homestead

THE OLDE ANGEL INN

Here, in the oldest operating inn in Canada and probably the most authentic recreation of a British pub on this side of the Atlantic, patrons
have the opportunity to enjoy a traditional pub-style meal (the menu includes such British fare as steak and kidney pie, bangers and mash, and fish
and chips served on newsprint) and a wide variety of local ales and wines.
Accommodations are available in rooms upstairs that ooze rustic charm or
in the adjacent Swayze's Cottage.

Location: 224 Regent Street
Phone: 905-468-3411
Email: angelinn@bellnet.ca
Website: angel-inn.com

GHOST SHIP *FOAM*

The seven young men who drowned aboard the *Foam* are interred in
St. Mark's Cemetery. Their resting place is marked by a white granite headstone (which has unfortunately suffered the ravages of time, so the original
inscription is illegible) and a modern bronze plaque that identifies the deceased and summarizes the story of their sad demise.

Location: Byron Street, east of King

QUEENSTON HEIGHTS

Most of the lands upon which the Battle of Queenston Heights unfolded
are today encompassed by beautiful parkland and preserved as a national
historic site. The highlight of the tranquil setting is Brock's Monument,
erected in 1853 (the original monument was bombed by a terrorist
in 1840), to commemorate the fallen hero. A tomb below contains his
remains, and a climb to the top affords unparalleled views of the Niagara
Region. Costumed staff members are often on hand to lead visitors on a
guided tour of the park, explaining how the battle unfolded and putting
it in historical context (interpretive markers located throughout the park

offer a self-guided option). Afterward, visitors can visit the gift shop or enjoy a fine meal at the restaurant.

Location: 14184 Niagara Parkway
Phone: 1-877-642-7275
Email: info@niagaraparks.com
Website: www.niagaraparks.com/visit/nature-garden/queenston-heights

LAKEFRONT GAZEBO

The Lakefront Gazebo at Queen's Royal Park is one of the most picturesque spots in Niagara-on-the-Lake, so don't forget to bring a camera. From this vantage point you have a terrific view of Lake Ontario and across the Niagara River to Fort Niagara in the United States. Sadly, there is nothing left to remind us of the existence of the elegant Queen's Royal Hotel or the important role it played in Niagara-on-the-Lake's development.

Location: 16 Front Street

PRINCE OF WALES HOTEL

With its century homes, quaint shops, and heritage sites, Niagara-on-the-Lake is perhaps the most historical community in the province. At its centre is the majestic Prince of Wales Hotel, a sophisticated and refined oasis of Victorian elegance filled with twenty-first-century comforts. Consistently ranked one of Ontario's finest hotels, it offers charm and romance in an intimate setting.

Enjoy a meal at Noble Restaurant, the hotel's world-class restaurant, which features the finest wines and flavours from across the Niagara Region, or perhaps indulge in the Victorian tradition of high tea in the elegant Drawing Room. Then pamper yourself at the Secret Garden Spa, newly renovated in 2008, with aesthetics, healing reflexology, or the hotel's trademark line of tea-based Specialtea treatments. If you want to feel spoiled, this is the place to do it.

Location: 6 Picton Street
Phone: 1-888-669-5566
Website: www.vintage-hotels.com/princeofwales

FORT MISSISSAUGA

Though you can see the stone tower and the earthworks surrounding it from the road, to truly appreciate Fort Mississauga you need to experience it up close and first hand. A pathway from the corner of Simcoe and Front Streets leads through the fairways of Niagara-on-the-Lake Golf Club. (Watch out for incoming balls!) While the stone blockhouse is stoutly sealed up, visitors are free to explore the earthworks, enter tunnels (one of which emerges onto the lake and to a spectacular view), and tour a subterranean powder magazine. Pretty soon, and with the assistance of several information markers, one begins to gain an appreciation for the history of these eerie ruins.

Location: 223 Queen Street
Phone: 905-468-6614
Email: ont-niagara@pc.gc.ca
Website: pc.gc.ca/en/lhn-nhs/on/fortgeorge/decouvrir-discover/
    fortmississauga

NIAGARA APOTHECARY

This historical building is probably the oldest continuously operating pharmacy in Canada, dispensing medicines for more than a century. The apothecary has been painstakingly restored to its original condition as it would have likely appeared in 1865. Many of the original bottles and jars, prescription books, display cases, pharmacists' utensils, and even account books have been recovered and are on display. Knowledgeable volunteers from the Ontario College of Pharmacists are on hand and dressed in period costume to educate the public. Best of all, there's no admission fee.

Location: 5 Queen Street
Phone: 905-468-3845

Email: niagaraapothecary@ocpinfo.com
Website: www.ocpinfo.com/extra/apothecary/index.html

OLD COURTHOUSE

This imposing and impressive structure is a National Historic Site, and parts are open to the public free of charge. Visitors are welcome to enter the main hall to view the dozens of historical photos lining the walls. They can also see recreated nineteenth-century courtrooms and council chambers. The highlight, however, is undoubtedly the holding cell; there's something eerily alluring about it. The Court House Theatre upstairs used to operate as part of the Shaw Festival during the summer months. One quirky detail of the courthouse remains a mystery to this day: no one knows whether the stone faces carved above the windows are portraits of persons of the time or merely whimsical creations.

Location: 26 Queen Street

PILLAR AND POST INN

There is a subdued elegance to the Pillar and Post Inn. From the moment you enter the lobby, with sunshine streaming in through the skylights and beautiful terra cotta tile floors, you know you're entering a hotel that blends relaxation and comfort with attentive service and subtle opulence. It's an enchanting combination.

The Pillar and Post's thirteen-thousand-square-foot 100 Fountain Spa is among the finest in Ontario, featuring a wide array of services, a heated indoor saltwater pool, and, most seductive, a romantic outdoor hot springs. Take in some fine dining at the Cannery Restaurant, or retire to the Vintages Wine Bar and Lounge, where you can enjoy drinks in the glow of a fireplace and snack on a pizza of your own design.

Location: 48 John Street West
Phone: 1-888-669-5566
Website: www.vintage-hotels.com/pillarandpost

MCFARLAND HOUSE

Here, at the fully restored home of John McFarland, visitors get a taste of living in the early nineteenth century. Costumed interpreters lead tours of the building and educate guests about the home, its owner, and the turbulent era in which he lived. Enjoy home-baked goods, ice cream, a glass of wine with a light lunch, or a cup of tea (there are thirty-five varieties to choose from) on the outdoor patio, surrounded by flower blooms and the tranquility of parkland. A highlight for gardeners is the heritage herb garden, reflecting a typical kitchen garden of the era.

Location: 15927 Niagara Parkway
Phone: 905-468-3322
Website: www.niagaraparks.com/visit/heritage/mcfarland-house

BUTLER'S BURIAL GROUND

Butler's Burial Ground is far more than just an old and relatively obscure family graveyard. This was the site of a War of 1812 skirmish known as the Action at Butler's Farm, where a small band of British-allied warriors ambushed and defeated a much larger force of American soldiers. The details of this action are described on a historical plaque, though sadly a modern subdivision has sprung up over the fields and woods in which the fighting took place, making it difficult to imagine the unfolding skirmish.

Location: South end of Butler Street, along a dirt trail

FORT GEORGE

Muskets and cannons roared and much blood was spilled during the War of 1812 — and plenty of the action was centred around Fort George. Its dramatic history has been recaptured as staff wander the grounds dressed in the costumes of the day. Visitors can tour the Soldiers' Barracks, where wives and children, like Sarah Ann, shared the same living space as the men, or the Officers' Quarters where upper-class English officers lived a much more elegant lifestyle. Other reconstructed buildings include blockhouses, a kitchen, a craftsman shop, and a guardhouse. A number of special events are held here throughout the year. Ghost Tours of Niagara conduct gripping nighttime tours of the fort several evenings each week from May through October, but book early as they sell out quickly.

FORT GEORGE

Location: 51 Queen's Parade
Phone: 905-468-6614
Email: ont-niagara@pc.gc.ca
Website: www.pc.gc.ca/en/lhn-nhs/on/fortgeorge

GHOST TOURS OF NIAGARA

Phone: 905-468-6621
Email: admin@niagaraghosts.com
Website: www.niagaraghosts.com

ST. MARK'S CEMETERY

St. Mark's Anglican Church is undoubtedly the most attractive church in Niagara-on-the-Lake. It's also the most historic, and you could easily spend an afternoon roaming through the cemetery's headstones and delving into the stories they hint at. The best way to do so is with a copy of *Stones, Saints and Sinners: Walking Tours of Niagara-on-the-Lake's Large Historic Cemeteries* by Donald Combe and Fred Habermehl. This invaluable and highly entertaining guide is available from local booksellers, or directly from the St. Mark's Archive Committee. Don't miss the two-hundred-year-old trenches!

Location: 41 Byron Street
Phone: 905-468-3123
Email: stmarks@cogeco.net
Website: stmarks1792.com

ACKNOWLEDGEMENTS

The material in this book is the result of more than a year of research into the various aspects surrounding the ghostly heritage of Niagara-on-the-Lake. It wouldn't have been possible if not for the contribution of numerous individuals, who we'd like to take the time to thank: Dianne Turner and the staff at Vintage Hotels, for their gracious hospitality and welcome assistance; Ron Dale at Parks Canada, a matchless resource for War of 1812 information; Rebecca Pascoe, curator-manager at McFarland House; the staff at the Buttery, who willingly shared their experiences with us; Clark Bernat of the Niagara Historical Museum, who provided many of the historical images that grace this book; Heather Gorman, site supervisor at the Laura Secord Homestead, for giving us a historical look at this amazing woman and her times; Daniel Cumerlato of Ghost Walks, who shared stories and has been an enthusiastic supporter of this book since the first edition was published back in 2009; and the staff at the Olde Angel Inn. In addition, and perhaps most especially, we'd like to thank those people who took the brave step of coming forward with their own accounts of the paranormal; this book is far stronger for their experiences.

PERSONAL ACKNOWLEDGEMENTS

MARIA DA SILVA

As an enthusiast of the paranormal, I find it fascinating when history can be connected with ghostly occurrences, once again adding probability to the existence of an afterlife. With Niagara-on-the-Lake being so rich in history, it seemed the more we researched the area's hauntings, the more we learned about the community's past — and the more we became convinced the ghost stories were, in fact, real.

I would like to thank all those who supported us in the project, as well as Andrew, for allowing me to share a love for this area and become connected to history in a way I never dreamed possible.

ANDREW HIND

As a historian, I feel compelled to draw attention to all those, past and present, who helped preserve Niagara-on-the-Lake's historic charm and kept alive the countless stories that took place in this unique community. The quaint town enjoyed by countless tourists today was made possible by their dedication and commitment. I'd also like to thank Dianne Turner of Vintage Hotels, who, during the course of writing this book, went from a contact to a friend valued by both Maria and me. Her efforts on our behalf, and her encouragement, are appreciated.

I'd also like to thank Maria. On the rare occasions when a writer is actually able to trace an idea directly to its source, it's only right we acknowledge it. *Ghosts of Niagara-on-the-Lake* was born of Maria's fascination with Niagara. All the memorable experiences I enjoyed during the process of researching and writing this book are thanks to her and the inspiration she provided. Thank you.

NOTES

INTRODUCTION

1. The Haudenosaunee and the Huron-Wendat, who inhabited much of present-day Central Ontario, were long-standing enemies. In 1648, the Haudenosaunee invaded Huron-Wendat territory. Two French Jesuit missionaries, Jean de Brébeuf (1593–1649) and Gabriel Lalemant (1610–1649), who had converted many Huron-Wendat people to Christianity, were captured and brutally tortured to death. Their mission, Sainte-Marie (today, the popular tourist attraction, Sainte-Marie Among the Hurons), was put to the torch. The Haudenosaunee assault was so fierce that the Huron-Wendat Nation virtually ceased to exist, and those who survived were driven from their traditional lands. In the 1650s, the Haudenosaunee invaded and wiped out the Neutral Nation, which had taken in many of the Huron-Wendat refugees.
2. The name *Niagara* is derived from the First Nations word *Onghiara* or *Oniawgarah*, meaning "thunder waters" (Niagara Parks).
3. Lieutenant Colonel John Butler commanded a renowned Loyalist corps, known as Butler's Rangers, during the American Revolution. He, his men, and their families were among the first settlers of Niagara-on-the-Lake. See chapter 12 for further details on Butler.

4. John Graves Simcoe (1752–1806) was the first lieutenant governor of Upper Canada (present-day Ontario). A career soldier, he led the Queen's Rangers, an elite light infantry corps, with much success during the American Revolution. He was named to the post of lieutenant governor in 1791. After initially making Newark the province's capital, he had second thoughts about the town's vulnerability to attack, and in 1796 moved the seat of government to York (now Toronto). Ill health prompted him to return to Britain later that year. He died in 1806.

5. For more information on Isaac Brock, see chapters 4 and 10, as well as Mary Beacock Fryer's *Bold, Brave, and Born to Lead: Major General Isaac Brock and the Canadas* (Toronto: Dundurn, 2004).

6. After capturing Niagara-on-the-Lake, Major General Henry Dearborn followed up his success by sending a large force to knock the British off the Burlington Heights. On June 5, 3,700 Americans camped at Stoney Creek for the night to rest before the assault. Rather than await the attack, the British launched a surprise attack with seven hundred men at 2:00 a.m. on June 6. The resulting battle was a confusing affair, with friend fighting friend under the cover of darkness. Although the battle was tactically a draw, it was, nonetheless, a strategic victory for Britain, as the Americans subsequently withdrew and cancelled their ambitious plans for the summer campaign.

CHAPTER 1: LAURA SECORD HOMESTEAD

1. James Secord was a merchant and ran a potashery, which made potash for fertilizer by leaching wood ash in iron pots and then evaporating the liquid. By 1812, he considered himself "in easy circumstances." The house was comfortable, the Secords had two servants, and they owned several properties.

2. James Secord served as a member of a militia "car brigade" of artillery drivers, a unit charged with transporting large field guns and their ammunition by horse. The weapons, horses, and wagons were

prized targets for the enemy, and, perhaps unsurprisingly, James was badly wounded during the Battle of Queenston Heights, shot through the shoulder and knee. His wounds were so severe that there was serious doubt he would even last through the night.

3. The Battle of Beaver Dams was fought on June 24, 1813. The Americans had assembled six hundred men to surprise and destroy the British at Beaver Dams. Thanks to Laura Secord's warning, British Lieutenant FitzGibbon detached men to watch the various routes, along which a force of 465 First Nations warriors had gathered. The resulting ambush saw the Americans defeated resoundingly; after three hours of fighting, one hundred Americans lay dead or wounded and the remainder surrendered their arms. Only fifty casualties were reported among the attacking First Nations force.

4. By the end of the war, the Secords' home had been plundered twice and most of their belongings had been stolen or damaged. The wounds James suffered at the Battle of Queenston Heights prevented him from ever walking properly again, and he no longer had the resources to continue his career as a merchant. During 1817, their fortunes plummeted to such an extent that James was forced to sell off much of his property just to support his family, which by now had expanded to include seven children.

    In 1828, James was appointed registrar of the Niagara District Surrogate Court, and in 1833 was promoted to the position of judge. It all sounded so prestigious, but while there was some influence attached to these positions, there was little in the way of money. The Secords' lot only improved when James was made a collector of customs at Chippewa in 1835, a lucrative posting that, for a time, allowed the family to enjoy a level of comfort they hadn't experienced in more than twenty years.

CHAPTER 2: THE OLDE ANGEL INN

1. There is no definitive proof that a Captain Colin Swayze ever served in Niagara during the War of 1812, but that name has been associated

with the ghost at the Olde Angel Inn for decades. David Ling, a previous owner, is reputed to have uncovered genealogical evidence of an officer of this name and even had correspondence with his descendants in England. This can't be confirmed. Clark Bernat, the curator of the Niagara Historical Museum, does confirm, however, that there were several Swayzes in the local militia and British Army.

2. The Upper Canada Abolition Act of 1793, supported by Lieutenant Governor Simcoe, freed any slave who came into Ontario (Upper Canada), and stipulated that any child born of a slave mother would be free at the age of twenty-five. Upper Canada became the first British territory to pass an anti-slavery act. Other Canadian provinces followed suit after 1800.

3. In the fall of 1813, the Americans invaded the Niagara Peninsula yet again and quickly captured Fort George and Newark. By December, however, they began to feel that their position was untenable and made plans to abandon the peninsula. The Americans decided to destroy Fort George to prevent it from falling back into British hands, and on December 10, burned Newark so that the community and its inhabitants could not offer the British soldiers shelter or sustenance. It had snowed all day and was bitterly cold. People were cast out into the elements with only what they could carry. One old woman, too feeble to walk, was wrapped in a blanket and discarded into a snow bank from which she watched as her home was razed. In all, four hundred women, children, and elderly men were turned out into the cold that evening with only the heat of their burning village to warm them. Only a single building out of 150 in town was left standing after the fires had died and the ashes cooled.

    Evidence of this traumatic period, as it pertains to the Olde Angel Inn, was recently unearthed during the renovation of Swayze's Cottage, a frame house built around 1820 that now accommodates overnight guests at the inn. It was discovered that charred timber had been used in its construction, and several artifacts — including a musket ball and American uniform buttons — were recovered.

4. John Ross advertised the inn for sale in the Niagara *Gleaner* on June 19, 1826. He described it as "that excellent tavern and stand known

by the sign of the Angel Inn ... at the corner of the Market Square."

5. Richard Howard sold the Angel Inn in 1845 when he purchased the Promenade (Howard's Hotel), another Niagara-on-the-Lake hotel which, unlike the Angel Inn, is no longer with us. The new proprietor of the Angel Inn was John Fraser, a Scottish innkeeper who changed the name to the Mansion House and later to the Fraser's Hotel. Fraser was the last individual to operate the inn in its traditional role as a tavern/hotel.

6. Her full account is posted on the Ontario Ghost and Hauntings Research Society (GHRS) (www.torontoghosts.org).

7. The American tourist, whose name has been withheld upon his request, corresponded with us via email in the autumn of 2007.

CHAPTER 3: GHOST SHIP *FOAM*

1. The names of the five friends who boarded the *Foam* that ill-fated day are W. Anderson, P. Braddon, J.H. Murray, V.H. Taylor, and C. Vernon.

2. These opinions are contemporary but unsourced, as quoted by Jean Baker in a July 2000 article for the Niagara Historical Society and found in the files of the Niagara Historical Museum. Apparently, various yachtsmen at the time expressed their misgivings about the *Foam*'s design, and the Toronto *Globe* suggested that there had been potential weaknesses in her seaworthiness owing to a flawed design.

3. There were other mysteries associated with the tragedy as well. Among them, why were the Toronto boys buried in St. Mark's Cemetery in Niagara-on-the-Lake rather than returned to their hometown to rest beside departed family members and where grieving loved ones could more easily pay their respects? Their graves can still be seen in St. Mark's Cemetery.

4. The *New York Times*, July 22, 1874, reported that two bodies belonging to victims of the *Foam* disaster washed up on shore on July 21, at a point almost directly opposite Niagara-on-the-Lake. Presumably, the corpses had spent almost two weeks in the water before they were discovered.

CHAPTER 4: QUEENSTON HEIGHTS

1. The War of 1812 had been simmering for some time. Since the early 1790s, Europe had been embroiled in the Napoleonic Wars, during which the two principal combatants, Britain and France, sought to hurt each other by interfering with the flow of commerce. The resulting embargoes hurt American traders as much as they did the warring countries, as shippers suffered the loss of vessels and cargo. In addition, the Royal Navy, chronically short of men, habitually impressed American seamen suspected of being British citizens to serve aboard British vessels.

   Then there was the question of British support for hostile Indigenous Peoples in the Northwest Territories. The United States was spreading westward in the early nineteenth century and butting up against Indigenous Peoples, who justifiably felt threatened by the expansionistic Americans. Many in the U.S. believed that Britain secretly supplied these nations with arms and encouragement as a means of blocking the expansion. In short, they felt that Britain, and not the Indigenous Peoples whose lands they coveted, was the principal obstacle in the way of their continued westward expansion.

2. General Brock was an aggressive and imaginative leader who felt that the best way to secure Canada was to launch pre-emptive attacks upon U.S. soil. While America slowly built up forces along the Niagara River, Brock surreptitiously gathered three hundred regulars, six hundred militiamen, and six hundred First Nations warriors at Fort Malden, opposite Detroit. He let a false document fall into American hands that suggested he had five thousand warriors under his command, leading Brigadier General William Hull, the governor of Ohio and commander of American forces at Fort Detroit, to believe his own two thousand men were vastly outnumbered.

   On August 15, Brock demanded Hull's surrender. Believing that he was opposed by a more numerous foe, and fearing a massacre if his men and the civilians huddled in the fort — including his own daughter and her two children — Hull surrendered the next day. The loss of Detroit and so large a force with barely a shot being fired in resistance sent shockwaves through the United States, and many felt Hull had sold out his country. Two years later, he was tried for cowardice and treason, convicted, and sentenced to death. Only his heroic service in the American Revolution spared him from execution.

3. While Brock is idolized as a hero in Canada, and with good reason, his death revealed a fatal flaw in his character: impetuousness. As a commanding general, he had no place serving at the forefront of a counterattack. That task should have been assigned to a subordinate, a junior officer more readily replaced should he fall in the assault as Brock did.

4. John Wool was one of the few officers on the American side who acquitted himself well in the fighting. In recognition of his leadership, he was promoted to major in the 29th Infantry in April 1813, and retired as a major general in 1863.

5. George Jarvis, a fifteen-year-old soldier in the 49th Foot, was closest to Brock when he died and was witness to his final moments. He recorded the events in the following manner: "Ere long he [Brock] was singled out by one of them [an American marksman], who, coming forward, took deliberate aim and fired; several of the men noticed the action and fired — but too late — and our gallant General fell on his side, within a few feet of where I stood. Running up to him I enquired, 'Are you much hurt, Sir?' He placed a hand on his breast and made no reply and slowly sunk down." Ernest A. Cruikshank, *Documentary History of the Campaigns upon the Niagara Frontier 1812–1814*, 146.

6. Major General Roger Hale Sheaffe was born in Boston on July 15, 1763. In 1778, a wealthy patron purchased an ensigncy for Sheaffe in the 5th Foot. With that regiment, he spent ten years in Canada, gaining wide exposure to the conditions of the Canadian frontier and an intimate knowledge of its geography. After a decade back in Britain, he returned to Canada in 1802 and remained there until the outbreak of the War of 1812. He was therefore the British officer most familiar with the land that would soon be the scene of so much bloodshed.

But while Sheaffe's local knowledge was a boon for Brock, he was also a liability due to deficient leadership qualities and lack of social graces. One event that reveals the man's weaknesses as a senior officer was a near-mutiny at Fort George in 1803 while Sheaffe held command. The situation was only prevented from turning violent by the timely arrival of Brock from York. Nevertheless, Sheaffe proved his worth at the Battle of Queenston Heights and he must be given much of the credit for the British victory. He died in 1851, proud to the end of his contribution to the defence of British North America.

7. The American soldiers held an erroneous view of the Haudenosaunee, viewing them as, in the words of Lieutenant Jared Wilson, "savages, greedy for plunder and thirsting for blood." Willson, "A Rifleman at Queenston," 374.

8. A precise account of the losses suffered by the Americans in the Battle of Queenston Heights has never been made. Estimates range from 160 total casualties to five hundred killed. Malcomson, *A Very Brilliant Affair*, 193.

CHAPTER 5: LAKEFRONT GAZEBO

1. David Cronenberg made use of many local landmarks as haunting locations for his film *The Dead Zone*. In addition to the Lakefront Gazebo, they include St. Mark's Cemetery and the Screaming Tunnel.

2. The year 1862 was a troubling one for Niagara-on-the-Lake. At that time, the ratepayers of Lincoln County voted to move the county seat and its many offices from Niagara-on-the-Lake to the rapidly growing community of St. Catharines. This move left residents of Niagara-on-the-Lake feeling wounded and concerned for their future, since the title of county seat brought not only prestige but also a fair degree of economic benefits. They were particularly perturbed because the community had invested heavily in a magnificent new courthouse that would now sit empty, and so the town felt it was in their right to demand financial compensation for their loss.

The provincial government sympathized with their grievance and demanded Lincoln County pay Niagara-on-the-Lake eight thousand dollars. Desperate to reinvigorate the community, town leaders partnered with the private sector and invested their money in the construction of a magnificent hotel along the shores of the Niagara River where it flows into Lake Ontario. This hotel became known as the Queen's Royal Hotel.

3. Field, *Bicentennial Stories of Niagara-on-the-Lake*, 56–58.

4. The tennis courts at the Queen's Royal Hotel, which were located parallel to Front Street between King and Regent, on land now used as a parking lot, were considered world-class and played host to national and international competitions. In fact, the facilities were so well regarded that the Championship of Canada was played there in August 1907. There were also first-rate bowling greens on the hotel grounds, located near King and Front Streets.

Toronto Saturday Night reported on the golf course in 1910: "Both courses at Niagara-on-the-Lake are beautifully situated and kept in fine condition. The turf is of the best and the putting greens are well looked after and are very good. The soil is sandy, so dries quickly after a rain. In the grounds of the Queen's Royal there is a very convenient and well-arranged clubhouse."

A walkway close to the water's edge led from the hotel to the nearby golf course, which was then known as Mississauga Links. These impressive sporting facilities were built during a twenty-five-thousand-dollar expansion of the hotel and its grounds during the 1880s.

In addition to wealthy vacationers, the Queen's Royal also played host to Saturday night dinner dances that were extremely popular with members of the upper crust society from Toronto, most coming by steamboat. A five-dollar ticket covered the steamboat fare and hotel board for the weekend. A yellow stage and a baggage wagon met all boats at the town docks.

Extravagant balls were also put on by the hotel to entertain the high-ranking, well-heeled officers who came to Niagara-on-the-Lake every year to participate in annual military manoeuvres (in most years, as many as ten thousand soldiers were involved). The most lavish of these balls was held in 1910, when Sir John French, a British general and one of the most powerful military men in the Empire, attended the training exercises.

5. This story is based upon the psychic impressions of a Niagara area medium who contacted us with her story in August of 2008. The woman claimed to have made a connection with the ghostly woman at Queen's Royal Park, and to have had a psychic conversation, during which the spirit related the tragic story we shared with our readers. It should be noted that we corresponded with the woman with a skeptical mind, taking her story with a grain of salt, but left believing she was being upfront and honest. The details in her account were such that she either had to be as intimately familiar with the history of the location as we have become after months of research, or she truly did converse with the spirit of someone who had experienced the hotel for herself. It's up to each reader to decide what their stance is on mediumship and its role in paranormal investigation.

6. Savoie, *Shadows of Niagara*, 63.

7. Ibid.

8. Ron Dale, who was the national project manager for the War of 1812 bicentennial for Parks Canada, discussed the possibility of military action having taken place at the site of Queen's Royal Park during an email exchange in October 2008. "The American landings took place considerably west of the location," he explained, "on the shores of Lake Ontario where the former rifle range is now ... there was, in fact, no fighting in Queen's Royal Park."

CHAPTER 6: PRINCE OF WALES HOTEL

1. This story is a dramatization based on the various versions we've been told. Whether it's based, in whole or in part, on folklore or fact is impossible to determine. However, as is the case with most enduring legends, it's probable that there's at least a kernel of truth to the story.

2. Camp Niagara, a massive summer militia training camp, primarily encompassed Butler's Barracks and the Commons. During the First World War, the camp expanded greatly to include other properties in and around Niagara-on-the-Lake. The golf course at Fort Mississauga, for example, was dug up to provide a venue for trench assault tactics. Between the years 1914 and 1918, tens of thousands of men passed through Camp Niagara, arriving as raw recruits and leaving as soldiers well-prepared for the horrors of modern combat.

3. The cornerstone bearing the date *1864* can still be seen from the sidewalk today. The Prince of Wales has gone through at least half a dozen name changes since then, including Long's Hotel, the Arcade Hotel, the Niagara House, O'Neill's Hotel, and the Arlington Hotel. The original hotel was built of polychrome brick in an architectural style that was of the Second French Empire, seen most clearly in its mansard roof.

4. The transformation of the hotel began in 1881 when it was rebuilt from the ground up. A report from the *Niagara County News* (Lewiston, New York) on July 22, 1881, noted that a large three-storey brick hotel was being built on the corner of King and Picton. This is the Prince of Wales as we know it today. The one question that remains unanswered is: What precipitated such extensive reconstruction? Was it fire, the bane of nineteenth-century hotels, or simply whim?

5. The exact date that the hotel became known as the Prince of Wales has yet to be determined. We know it was operating under the name Niagara Hotel as late as July 24, 1919, when an article in the Niagara *Advance* made passing reference to "the well patronized Niagara Hotel." It's believed that Edward, the Prince of Wales, may have been expected to visit Niagara in the autumn of 1919 or perhaps in 1920. It seems likely that the hotel was hastily renamed in anticipation of his arrival and in honour of the previous Royal visit of 1901.

6. Ron Dale, email correspondence, October 2008.

7. Ron Dale, interview, October 2008.

8. There may be a second soul unable to escape from the bonds that tie her to the Prince of Wales. A few sources mention an apparition of an elderly woman that has been seen within the building, though no one we interviewed had any knowledge of such a ghost.

CHAPTER 7: FORT MISSISSAUGA

1. Niagara-on-the-Lake Golf Club is itself historic, being the first golf club in Ontario and the oldest existing golf course in North America. It was founded in 1875 by John Geale Dickenson, a resident of Niagara-on-the-Lake who lived across the road from the grounds. The golf club also holds the distinction of having hosted the first international tournament in North America, pitting Canadians against Americans on September 5–7, 1895.

2. At one point, Fort Mississauga included barracks, a guardroom, and cells. The centrepiece of the fort was the artillery-proof central tower, which housed a storeroom and magazine, living space for thirty-four men and their families, and a roof-top artillery battery. The tower wouldn't be completed until 1823, while the fort itself was never finished due to rising costs. Originally, it was intended to be a massive fortress, larger even than Fort George and home to more than a thousand troops. In fact, if the ambitious plans for Fort Mississauga had ever been realized, it would have been one of the largest forts in Canada.

   The central tower was planned as a barrack, an artillery battery, and a place of refuge and final defence should the fort be overrun. Only a determined enemy with heavy cannon, or a lengthy siege, could bring about its surrender. The tower measures fifty feet by fifty feet, with walls standing twenty-five feet high and eight feet thick. A reinforced platform on the roof, added in 1838, held a cannon with a range of 1.6 kilometres and the capability of reaching the American shore or bombarding vessels entering the Niagara River.

3. Under the orders of Lieutenant Governor Peter Hunter, a stone lighthouse was constructed by John Symington in 1804 to aid

navigation on Lake Ontario, specifically for vessels entering the Niagara River. It was the first lighthouse anywhere on the Great Lakes. The keeper, Dominick Henry, played an active part during the war. He and his wife assisted British soldiers who had been injured during the fighting on May 27, 1813, when Americans captured Niagara-on-the-Lake. In 1814, the lighthouse was destroyed to make way for Fort Mississauga, and material from the lighthouse was utilized in the construction of the new fort.

4. Fort Mississauga was garrisoned by British Regulars consistently until 1826. For a decade it was abandoned, except for use as a training ground by militia units. Repaired and rearmed following the Rebellion of 1837, it continued to be maintained and garrisoned by British troops until 1854, in response to border disputes with the United States. It was manned during the American Civil War and the Fenian scare of 1877, in both cases to ward off cross-border assaults that never materialized. By 1870, the fort was no longer considered of military value and was abandoned, save for periodic use by Canadian militia units.

5. The closest Fort Mississauga came to being attacked occurred in July of 1814, when an American brigade of three thousand men, commanded by Colonel Moses Porter, advanced against it. Facing earthworks that were formidable despite not yet being completed, and under fire from powerful long-range guns, the American attack was half-hearted at best, and Porter quickly withdrew his men from the field of battle.

6. Whether the story of the flogged soldier is fact or folklore is unknown. It's certainly possible that the events did occur as recorded, as flogging was a common practice in the British army during the Napoleonic Wars era, even for relatively minor offences. A soldier could, and often did, survive thirty lashes for minor crimes, but serious offences resulted in as many as two hundred lashes, a punishment that was generally fatal.

7. Andrew Greenhill, "Narrative of the Volunteer Camp at Niagara, June 1871," *Canadian Military History* 12, no. 4 (2003): 37–54.

8. Interview conducted October 2008.

9. Nicole volunteered her creepy experience with the authors via email correspondence in September 2005.

10. Chief John Norton (c. 1770–1830), known as Teyoninhokarawen in his native tongue, was one of the principal chiefs of the Haudenosaunee Confederacy. His father was Cherokee and his mother was Scottish, and Norton was raised and educated in Britain. After a brief military career as a soldier in the British army, he became a teacher, fur trader, and interpreter for the Indian Department.

    Norton must be given some of the credit for the victory at the Battle of Queenston Heights. He and eighty warriors arrived on scene during the confusion after General Brock's death and when British fortunes were at their lowest ebb. "Comrades and brothers," he said to his handful of warriors, "be men." He then led them up the escarpment to face the enemy, almost a thousand strong. Their presence caused fear to spread through the enemy ranks and kept the invaders occupied at a critical stage in the battle. Norton and his followers prevented the invaders from consolidating their position, giving the British time to prepare the counterstrike that ultimately won the battle.

11. At least five First Nations warriors were killed on the day of the Battle of Queenston Heights, but sources don't mention the exact number or specifically where they died. Since British casualties for that day included dead and wounded at Fort George and at other points along the Niagara River, it's reasonable to assume that the same applied for First Nations casualties as well. It's therefore possible that the legend bears some truth and that a First Nations person was, in fact, beheaded by a cannonball on the site of Fort Mississauga.

CHAPTER 8: NIAGARA APOTHECARY

1. The family, who wished for their names to be withheld, shared this story with the authors via email in July 2006.

2. The Ontario Heritage Foundation (OHF) acquired the Niagara Apothecary from the local Niagara Foundation and proceeded to both

finance and spearhead its restoration. One of Canada's most noted restoration architects, Peter Stokes, who lived close to the apothecary, supervised the meticulous work. The apothecary was opened again as a museum in 1971. The Ontario College of Pharmacists (OCP) accepted the responsibility of restoring the professional practice aspects in order to ensure the museum accurately reflected an operating pharmacy of the 1860s. The college also agreed with the OHF to operate the apothecary as a museum for an initial period of thirty-five years (until 2005). This agreement has been extended.

3. For more information on Judge Campbell, see chapter 9.

4. Tim shared his experiences with the authors via email in May 2006.

5. Henry Paffard was the third pharmacist in Niagara-on-the-Lake, but the first to operate from the building known today as the Niagara Apothecary. He was an apprentice to James Harvey, and when Harvey died suddenly in the autumn of 1851, Paffard briefly operated the pharmacy for Harvey's widow. In 1852, he bought and took over the business and hired on his nineteen-year-old brother Charles as an apprentice. In 1868, he purchased the office of lawyer, and later judge, E.C. Campbell, made extensive renovations, and moved the business to its present location. Paffard remained the village pharmacist until 1898.

6. Henry Paffard's apprentice and successor was John de Witt Randall, who served as village pharmacist from 1898 to 1914. In addition to operating his business, Randall also served as lord mayor of Niagara-on-the-Lake from 1907 to 1909, and then again in 1912, and was chosen as chief magistrate in 1913. He was known to have had rather strong opinions about matters relating to the town, and wasn't above overriding the views of his own town council when it suited his purposes. Naturally enough, his personal method of achieving results did not seem to be appreciated by other elected officials working with him.

Randall took ill unexpectedly in the pharmacy on March 12, 1914, went home early, and, after what was described as "paralysis of the brain" — likely a stroke — he died at 4:30 that afternoon. Randall's funeral appeared to prompt flags at half-mast in the whole town on public buildings and private homes, and a capacity crowd in the church.

Two men followed Randall as pharmacist. Arthur James Coyne ran the business from 1914 to 1920. Coyne also operated a second pharmacy at 116 Lake Street, St. Catharines. When the restored Niagara Apothecary was dedicated and opened in May 1971, A.J. Coyne and his wife and other members of their family were present. At that time, Coyne was still practising in St. Catharines at his original pharmacy, but retired not long after. Erland William Field, a native of Virgil, had apprenticed with Randall and graduated from the OCP School in 1913. Field enlisted in the Canadian Army Medical Corps on June 21, 1915, at Camp Niagara and served overseas as part of the Fifth Canadian Field Ambulance, and then the First Canadian Clearing Station in 1917. After the war, he became an executive member of the local legion at its founding meeting in 1928. Declining health persuaded Field to close the pharmacy in 1964. He died a year later, but not before he had agreed that the OCP and Niagara Foundation would have first rights of purchase for the pharmacy.

CHAPTER 9: OLD COURTHOUSE

1. The first courthouse was built in 1795, near the corner of King and Prideaux Streets. During the war, as many as three hundred prisoners, most of them political offenders and disloyal citizens, were confined here. The second courthouse was built in 1816 where Rye Park stands today. After the third courthouse was constructed, the building was converted into Our Western Home, opening in 1869 — an institution where impoverished girls from Britain were brought to be trained in domestic skills and then placed in area households as servants. The facility was closed in 1913 and the buildings were demolished.

2. The old courthouse served as Niagara-on-the-Lake's town hall until 1972, when the city was amalgamated with Niagara Township and

centralized town offices were built in Virgil. A few years earlier, in 1962, the Shaw Festival celebrated its inaugural season with performances in the upper floors of the old courthouse. The historic building was restored in 1981 as the town's bicentennial project, and today it houses a refurbished Lord Mayor's Chambers and holding cell (both open to the public), a 327-seat theatre, the Chamber of Commerce, and offices for Parks Canada.

3. Edward Clarke Campbell was an important figure in mid-nineteenth-century Niagara-on-the-Lake. Born in 1806, he was the son of Donald Campbell, fort major of Fort George, and later the protege of local lawyer Robert Dickson, whose offices were located where the Niagara Apothecary stands today. Campbell became Dickson's partner, was elected a member of Parliament in 1840 (by a mere one vote over H.J. Boulton), and a year later was made a judge.

    In addition to a fine distinguished legal career, Campbell "took great interest in many ways in the prosperity of the town." He was, for example, prominent in St. Andrew's Church congregation, was a founding member and later long-time president of the Niagara Mechanics' Institute (the forerunner of the library), and was active in horticultural circles.

4. Daniel Cumerlato is well-respected in his field, serving as a consultant and paranormal investigator for the television shows *Creepy Canada* and *Ghost Trackers*. He also offers guided tours of historically haunted locales, including Niagara-on-the-Lake. For more information, visit the Ghost Walks website at www.ghostwalks.com.

5. This account was shared with the authors via phone interview in August 2008.

CHAPTER 10: PILLAR AND POST INN

1. During the First World War, Poland did not exist as an independent country, as Germany and Russia occupied the territory historically considered part of this nation. The Allies decided to form an army of émigré Poles from Canada and the United States, offering them

a homeland in exchange for fighting in the killing fields of France against the Germans. Thousands of eager and patriotic Poles responded to the call to arms and were trained in Niagara. Even today, these soldiers are remembered fondly in Niagara-on-the-Lake.

2. The transformation of the Pillar and Post from a canning factory to an elite hotel took place over thirty years. In 1972, it opened its doors for the first time as a thirty-five-room inn. Renovations and restoration occurred again in 1974, 1980, and, most extensively, in 1994 (which brought the room total to 122). The time and money was well spent; in 1999, the Pillar and Post was voted Best Country Inn in Canada by readers of *Canadian Country Inns* magazine, and in the spring of 2000 was bestowed the esteemed Four Diamond Award for accommodations by the CAA.

3. The presence of a young girl in what was once an industrial facility perplexed us. She seemed so out of place, and we were troubled by the fact that she would be bound specifically and exclusively to the part of the Pillar and Post that encompasses the old canning factory. Then we stumbled upon a personal account of a woman relating her childhood experiences that seemed to shed light on the matter: "Seasonal jobs could be had at the canning factory. While our mothers worked peeling fruit, we children liked to help put the empty cans down the chute. For a change, we watched the firemen shovelling peach pits into the blazing fire" (Field 124).

Is it possible that the ghostly young girl came to work with her mother and met an untimely demise within the canning factory? In all likelihood, we'll never know for certain, but suddenly her presence seems to make more sense — and is sadder in its implications.

Some sources say it's actually a woman dressed in a white, 1920s-style dress that's spotted walking down the stairs in front of the restaurant, only to disappear before reaching the bottom. This is an example of how stories evolve and become distorted with each telling. Everyone we spoke to — every source well-versed in local lore and all staff at the Pillar and Post — was unanimous in their assertion that the ghost is a young girl, perhaps ten years of age, and not an adult woman.

4. All quotes from staff were provided during a visit by the authors in October 2008.

5. This account, and many more from across the province, can be found on the website of the Toronto and Ontario Ghosts and Hauntings Research Society at www.torontoghosts.org.

6. No one knows for certain how old this painting of Lieutenant Colonel Butler is, and therefore whether he truly was fond of it.

7. Interestingly enough, Room 222 is almost directly above Room 118. Is this evidence of an energy vortex that serves to attract spirits or weaken the veil between the realms of the dead and the living?

8. This account can be found on the Toronto and Ontario Ghost and Haunting Research Society's website at www.torontoghosts.org.

CHAPTER 11: CORKS RESTAURANT

1. John Robert Colombo, in his book *Mysterious Ontario*, cites the date for these tragic events as April 7, 1850. This has yet to be confirmed by any primary documentation, so must remain suspect until such time as it can be independently verified.

2. Some sources claim Philip fled Niagara-on-the-Lake and was never seen again, presumably living out his life in anonymity. Others suggest that he was captured during his panicked flight and stretched at the end of a rope by a party of vigilantes seeking justice. The truth has yet to be definitively determined.

3. There are a few references to another ghost in the King Henry VIII Feast, said to be that of a small child. Sometimes it's identified as a boy, other times as a girl. No one that the authors spoke to had any knowledge of this spirit or who this ghost might be — assuming it does, in fact, exist.

CHAPTER 12: MCFARLAND HOUSE

1. The building's history between the time of John McFarland's death and 1959, when the Niagara Parks Commission opened it to the public, is somewhat sketchy. The home remained in the McFarland family for more than a century, and in the late 1930s was purchased by Niagara Parks from the last living direct descendant of John McFarland. The Second World War interrupted plans to restore the building, so it remained vacant throughout the 1940s and 1950s. By this point, it had become run down and required extensive repair. Renovations took more than two years to complete. Further restoration work was done in 1973.

2. There is little evidence that John McFarland performed the duties of a boatbuilder in Niagara (he was listed as a yeoman), so the land granted by the Crown would have been a reward for services rendered prior to coming to Canada, likely as a shipbuilder at a Royal Navy Dockyard in England. The land deeded to McFarland included lots 21, 22, 23, and later 65, in the Township of Niagara — a total of 608 acres. There is speculation that he had a wealthy relative who provided the initial financing for his additional land purchases and the construction of his impressive home only two years after being deeded the property.

3. The home was built from red bricks made at a kiln located on the McFarland property. As originally constructed, it would have consisted of only the front, rectangular portion we see today. A back wing was added later in the nineteenth century in order to accommodate the needs of a growing family. The exact year in which this addition was built is a matter of some controversy: some sources suggest it was as early as the 1820s, others indicate it was likely much later in the nineteenth century.

4. The children of John McFarland are (in order of birth): John, James, Martha, Ann, Jane, Sarah, Duncan, Marjory, and Mary. Interestingly, Ann McFarland would marry John Wilson, her stepmother's brother.

5. There are two versions of the events that conspired to see John McFarland incarcerated as a prisoner of war. In the first, American

officers arrived upon his doorstep and inquired whether he would be willing to give up his home for their use as a hospital. When he answered with a curt "no," he was quickly deemed hostile and taken prisoner. The second version saw John McFarland and his second-eldest son, James, working in the fields one day, when three American soldiers happened upon the scene. The invaders tried to seize a pair of horses, but were chased away by John and James wielding fence rails as clubs. Unfortunately, the soldiers returned with reinforcements and not only took the horses but took John and James prisoner as well.

James later escaped from captivity and, while returning to Canada, made a point of memorizing the troop strength and defences at Fort Niagara, as well as the lay of the surrounding land. He stole a boat, rowed across the river, and gave the information to the commander at Fort George. Armed with this invaluable information, the British raided and captured Fort Niagara on December 19, 1813. In fact, the British force assembled on the McFarland property and boarded their boats in a ravine just behind McFarland House.

6. Niagara Historical Society pamphlet, as quoted by Rebecca Pascoe, manager-curator of McFarland House.

7. Account provided via email, August 2008.

8. Martha posted her experiences on the message boards of the Toronto and Ontario Ghosts and Hauntings Research Society at www.torontoghosts.org.

9. During a November 2008 email exchange, Rebecca Pascoe elaborates on her thoughts about the story of American soldiers being buried on the property:

> The issue of military burial is a tricky one, and the answer to that so-often-posed question, "Are there people buried on [this] piece of property X which was related to the War of 1812?" actually depends on many factors: Were there mass casualties involved? Was it possible to transport the dead to a local church-yard? Did you want to bother transporting the dead

to the local churchyard? (i.e., Were they part of "your" army — or were they the enemy?)

The best that any of us can say regarding the issue of military graves on the McFarland property is that while we do not know for sure, it is possible. Although many military documents of the time period do mention the home being used as a cannon battery, hospital, and headquarters, there are no specific notations (that we are aware of, at least) of the property serving a double purpose as a graveyard. However, since the house was used as a military hospital and logic would dictate not all patients survived their wounds, then, yes, it is possible that soldiers died here and are, in fact, buried on the property.

10. Account provided via phone interview, October 2008.

CHAPTER 13: BUTLER'S BURIAL GROUND

1. John Butler saw considerable action during the Seven Years' War (1756–1763), the last and most decisive of a long series of confrontations among the French, British, First Nations, and colonists for control of North America. The war effectively ended with British victory at the Plains of Abraham (Quebec City) and the conquest of Canada in 1759, though a formal peace took another four years to materialize. Engagements John Butler fought at include: Lake George (September 8, 1755), Fort Carillon (July 8, 1758), the capture of Fort Frontenac (August 26, 1758), and the campaigns around Fort Niagara (June–July 1759) and Montreal (September 1760). His record was one of notable distinction.

There were over one hundred officers and interpreters, including Butler, in the Indian Department, serving with various First Nations Peoples and in frontier forts. Their role was to ensure good relations continued between British authorities and the First

Nations Peoples and, in the time of war, to secure their alliance against the Americans so that they fight on their side. Officers were involved in scores of skirmishes as well as several large-scale battles, sometimes leading the First Nation contingents.

2. Howard Swiggett, *War Out of Niagara: Walter Butler and the Tory Rangers* (Cranbury, NJ: Scholar's Bookshelf, 2005).

3. The first major action for the Rangers occurred in the spring of 1778, when Butler led a force of two hundred Rangers and three hundred warriors against Wyoming Valley, Pennsylvania. While several small forts in the Wyoming Valley surrendered, a major rebel force retreated into Forty Fort and proved too strong to dislodge. Knowing he could not take the fort by direct assault, Butler had his Rangers feign a retreat to lure the rebels out. The enemy took the bait, walked into an ambush, and was decimated. Butler's legend was born.

    In addition to the Cherry Valley Massacre (November 11, 1778), the Rangers conducted brutal raids into New York's Schoharie Valley (October 15–19, 1780) and Mohawk Valley (summer 1781), and in 1782, put the town of Wheeling, West Virginia, to the torch.

4. John Butler was a towering figure in Niagara-on-the-Lake. He served as deputy superintendent of the Indian Department of Niagara, justice of the peace, member of the Land Board of Niagara, commander of the Nassau and Lincoln County militia, leader of the Church of England, and a member of the local Masonic Order. He was embittered, though, that no senior government post was offered to him despite his lengthy service to the Crown.

5. Many of the tombstones at Butler's Burial Ground have been lost to time and vandals. Even John Butler has no headstone, and the exact location of this grave is unknown. This makes it difficult to determine exactly who lies in the cemetery, and specifically how many former Rangers. We know of at least four who served in the ruthless Loyalist Corps: John Butler, his son Thomas (1756–1812), Rolfe Clench, and John Freel. In addition, there was a Claus on the rolls of the Rangers.

    After John Butler, Clench is perhaps the most noteworthy figure. Born in Pennsylvania in 1762, he served as a lieutenant in Butler's

Rangers from July 1782. After the war, he settled on the corner of what is now Johnson and Mississauga Streets in Niagara-on-the-Lake (his second home, located at 234 Johnson Street, is still there), and served in a number of prominent positions: clerk of the peace, the community's first town clerk, clerk of the Land Commission, judge of the Surrogate Court, and member of the provincial legislature. He died in 1828 and was buried at Butler's Burial Ground. Later, his will was uncovered, clearly specifying that he wished to be buried beside his daughter Eweratta, who died in 1797 and was buried at St. Mark's Cemetery. As per his wishes, Clench's body was disinterred and moved to St. Mark's, where he lies beside his beloved daughter.

6. Janet Carnochan, "Graves and Inscriptions in the Niagara Peninsula," *Niagara Historical Society* 10 (1902): 1–72.

7. According to Ron Dale, the crypt was buried in sand to preserve the stonework and prevent rampant vandalism. "The cemetery has, until recently, been poorly tended and those laid to rest therein treated with little respect. By the late nineteenth century, the fences around the burial ground had been removed, the plots overgrown, and cattle allowed to graze between the headstones. Janet Carnochan complained of its condition, and the early Queen Victoria Parks Commission repaired the crypt," explains Dale. "Broken tomb-stones on the property and any remains from inside the crypt were concentrated in one area on the hill, where they remain. The crypt was closed with an iron grill gate but vandals kept breaking in, so eventually a steel plate was welded in place. A few years ago, prior to burying the crypt in sand, the plate was removed to assess the condition of the interior of the crypt. It was found to be completely empty so we must assume that the Parks people removed anything when they did the work around 1909."

William Claus had the crypt built in the late 1790s to hold his remains and those of his family. Born in 1765, Claus was the son of British army colonel Daniel Claus, an agent with the Indian Department. William followed his father into Indian Department service, rising to the rank of deputy superintendent by the War of 1812. Though he was a prominent and respected citizen of

Niagara-on-the-Lake, Claus abused his position of authority among the First Nations Peoples to line his pockets with gold. At the time, First Nations people in Upper Canada (Ontario) were forbidden to sell their property without first consulting his department. Claus was known to have profited largely on bribes from prospective owners, since his was the final say in any proposed sale.

William died in 1826 after a long battle with cancer and was buried in the family vault beside his mother, who had died in 1801. Two of Claus's sons followed him into service in the British army and predeceased him: Lieutenant William Claus served at Waterloo and died in India in 1824, and Lieutenant Daniel Claus died in 1813 at the Battle of Crysler's Farm. Claus's home, the Wilderness, still stands at 407 King Street in Niagara-on-the-Lake.

8. Savoie, *Shadows of Niagara*, 63.

9. Interestingly, ghostly phenomenon is not limited to the boundaries of the burial ground. The sights and sounds of spectral battle are occasionally heard in the surrounding woods and in the modern subdivision that backs onto Butler's Burial Ground — other worldly reminders of a skirmish known as the Action at Butler's Farm. On July 8, 1813, an outpost of the American army encamped near Fort George was ambushed and defeated by warriors led by Chiefs John Norton and Blackbird, and Indian Department interpreters Michel Brisebois, Louis Langlade, and Barnet Lyons. Lieutenant Samuel Eldridge and twenty-two soldiers of the 13th United States Infantry were killed during the engagement and a dozen were taken prisoner.

CHAPTER 14: SARAH ANN AND OTHER FORT GEORGE GHOSTS

1. Kyle Upton is the founder and owner of Niagara Ghost Tours, which offers guided nighttime tours of Fort George that blend history and ghosts into a wonderfully entertaining commentary. Having volunteered and worked at Fort George for a number of years, Kyle determined that a ghost tour was a great way to expose people to its

history. In 1994, with the blessing of Parks Canada, Kyle founded Niagara Ghost Tours.

2. Phone interview with Kyle Upton, October 2008.

3. Though some of its wooden buildings were rebuilt after the War of 1812, Fort George became all but obsolete. As the construction of nearby Fort Mississauga continued, along with a complex of storehouses and barracks known today as Butler's Barracks, both of which were out of range of American guns at Fort Niagara, they soon eclipsed Fort George in military importance. By the 1820s, Fort George was no longer being used regularly, and the buildings were becoming decrepit. Following the Rebellion of 1837, some cavalry were posted there, but the renewed occupation was both small in scale and short-lived. By 1867, the buildings either collapsed or had been scavenged over for lumber by locals. Ultimately, the site became a farmer's field.

4. The stories involving ghostly encounters with Sarah Ann are provided courtesy of Kyle Upton and appear in various forms in his book *Niagara's Ghosts 2*.

5. Fort George was largely abandoned by the British military soon after the War of 1812, so how was it that Sarah Ann came to live at Fort George? The answer lies in another Canadian conflict, the 1837 Upper Canada Rebellion. In that year, the fiery newspaper man, politician, and rabble-rouser William Lyon Mackenzie, supported by elements in the United States, led a rebellion against the government of Upper Canada to secure greater political, social, and economic rights for the common man. Though his rebellion was quickly crushed at the Battle of Montgomery's Tavern and a handful of other minor actions, Mackenzie escaped and established a rebel government on Navy Island in the Niagara River. As a result, there was renewed military presence in Niagara, including a detachment of cavalry that used the decaying grounds of Fort George for grazing. When Thomas Tracey, the troop sergeant major with the King's Dragoon Guards, was posted here, he brought his family with him.

6. The stone to Sarah Ann is located on the left-hand side of St. Mark's Cemetery. It reads: "In memory of Sarahann, daughter of

Hannah and Thomas B. Tracey, Troop Serjeant Major in the Kings Dragoon Guards. Who died on the 19th of July, 1840 in the 7th year of her age."

CHAPTER 15: ST. MARK'S CEMETERY

1. The story of Brock's Rock, also known as Brock's Seat, is a mixture of fact and folklore. It's a matter of record that, during the opening months of the War of 1812, Major General Isaac Brock would spend hours down by the Niagara River, sitting on a rock along the shoreline and gazing across to the United States. His thoughts were consumed with when and where the inevitable American attack would materialize, and how he would counter the invasion. It was here, on a rock by the shore, as much as in any headquarters or military encampment, that he laid out his strategy for the war. But while we know for sure that Brock would sit upon a rock, no one knows if it was, in fact, this particular rock.

   Local resident William Kirby was certain that the rock we know today as Brock's Seat was the stone upon which Brock sat. When he learned that a large dock was to be built along the river, and much of the shoreline altered to accommodate it, he grew concerned for the safety of this link to the Canadian hero. To preserve it, Kirby had the rock brought to St. Mark's Cemetery, the only place where he was sure it would remain safe. It remains there today.

2. When the church was built in 1792, there had already been a cemetery on site for many years. The exact date of founding is unknown. The first headstone we know of dates to 1782, but it's possible that some stones may have predated the church and been lost to the ravages of time and the elements. When established, it served as a graveyard for all denominations, and was the only public cemetery in town until the 1830s (though there were a number of private burial grounds). The headstones at St. Mark's reveal the names of many well-known and important political, social, and clerical leaders from Niagara-on-the-Lake and across the province.

The grounds occupied by St. Mark's Cemetery had been used as a burial ground by First Nations people long before Europeans arrived. In fact, there are places within the cemetery where no bodies have been interred and no construction has taken place simply because it's believed bodies are buried there. For example, a diviner concluded that between the markers to the veterans of the World Wars and the Parish Hall lie at least seven graves of non-Europeans of relatively recent vintage, probably dating to the late eighteenth or very early nineteenth century. Some surmise that these may be the bodies of Haudenosannee warriors killed at the Battle of Queenston Heights.

3. The first stone in St. Mark's Cemetery, bearing the name Leonard Blanck, and dating back to 1782, is preserved within the church itself. It was unearthed during excavation either when the church transepts were added in 1839 or when the Sunday schoolhouse was built in 1896. It is among the oldest known headstones in Ontario. Unfortunately, no one knows who Leonard Blanck is. It's been suggested that he was a French explorer or fur trader named Blanc or Leblanc. Some records refer to a First Nations chief named Blank; might this stone mark his grave? It's also possible that no one knew the deceased's surname, and called him Leonard Blank in much the same way we would use John Doe. Of course, there are Blancks living in Niagara-on-the-Lake, so Leonard might simply be an unknown member of this family tree.

4. During the War of 1812, St. Mark's Anglican Church was used as a hospital by the British to treat the mass casualties from the Battle of Queenston Heights as well as other engagements. Later, during the American occupation, it was used as a commissary to store and prepare food. Along with the rest of Niagara-on-the-Lake, St. Mark's was burned by the Americans before their retreat in December 1813. The stout stone walls resisted the flames, but the roof and interior were completely consumed by flames and destroyed.

The scars of this traumatic period can still be seen in the cemetery. Rifle pits and trenches dug by the Americans as part of their defences can still be seen in amongst the gravestones. It's believed that these trenches were shored up with headstones pulled from the cemetery, which might explain why so few from the pre-1812 era exist.

5.   There is some controversy over the nature and cause of the marks on the tombstones. While the notion that the stones were used as impromptu operating tables for amputations is the most widespread and likely explanation, there are two other schools of thought. Some believe it's possible that, since the church had also been used by the Americans as a commissary to store and prepare food, the stones had been used as chopping blocks and the disfiguring cuts were made by the cleavers of the military cooks. Another school of thought suggests that the cuts were made by American soldiers with their bayonets, disfiguring the graves of individuals they found offensive.

6.   The nighttime investigation of John Savoie and Pauline Raby yielded other results. A tape recorder picked up breathing and someone saying, "Help me, help us, help us." The recorder also picked up the words "head came off " immediately after Raby felt the distinct sensation of head trauma. Was she contacting a wounded soldier sent here for medical treatment? Other times, the recorder picked up barked commands such as "get moving" and "get down," which might be related to the period when American trenches were dug in the cemetery to serve as defensive works. While at the disfigured tombstones, Raby had the thought that "someone is trying to do something on top of it and whatever it is does not feel good," and began to feel great physical pain (Savoie 61–62).

7.   Account provided via email, February 2006.

8.   Account provided via phone interview, October 2006.

BIBLIOGRAPHY

Baker, Jean. "The *Foam*." Article for the Niagara Historical Society.

Benn, Carl. *The War of 1812*. London: Osprey, 2002.

Carnochan, Janet. "Graves and Inscriptions in the Niagara Peninsula." *Niagara Historical Society* 10 (1902): 1–72.

———. *History of Niagara*. Belleville, ON: Mika, 1973. First published 1914.

Chartrand, René. *Loyalist American Troops 1775–1784*. London: Osprey, 2008.

Collins, Gilbert. *Guidebook to the Historic Sites of the War of 1812*. Toronto: Dundurn Press, 1998.

Colombo, John Robert. *Mysteries of Ontario*. Toronto: Hounslow, 1999.

Cruikshank, Ernest A., ed. *Documentary History of the Campaigns upon the Niagara Frontier 1812–1814*. Welland, ON: Tribune Press, 1896.

Dale, Ronald J. *Niagara-on-the-Lake: Its Heritage and Its Festival*. Toronto: James Lorimer, 1999.

Field, John L., ed. *Bicentennial Stories of Niagara-on-the-Lake*. Niagara-on-the-Lake: Niagara-on-the-Lake Bicentennial Committee, 1981.

Habermahl, Fred. *St. Mark's Storied Past*. Niagara-on-the-Lake: St. Mark's Archive Committee, 2006.

Habermahl, Fred, and Donald L. Combe. *St. Mark's: Persons of Hopeful Piety*. Niagara-on-the-Lake: St. Mark's Archive Committee, 2000.

————. *Stones, Saints and Sinners: Walking Tours of Niagara-on-the-Lake's Large Historic Cemeteries*. Niagara-on-the-Lake: St. Mark's Archive Committee, 1995.

Hauck, Dennis William. *The International Directory of Haunted Places*. London: Penguin, 2000.

Kirby, William. *Annals of Niagara*. Niagara Falls, ON: Lundy's Lane Historical Society, 1972. First published in 1896.

Kohn, George Childs. *Dictionary of Wars*. New York: Checkmark, 1999.

MacDonald, Cheryl. *Laura Secord: The Heroic Adventures of a Canadian Legend*. Canmore, AB: Altitude, 2005.

Malcomson, Robert. *A Very Brilliant Affair*. Toronto: Robin Brass Studio, 2003.

Merritt, Richard, Nancy Butler, and Michael Powers, eds. *The Capital Years: Niagara-on-the-Lake, 1792–1796*. Niagara-on-the-Lake: Niagara Historical Society, 1991.

Pulsifer, Cameron. "Narrative of the Volunteer Camp at Niagara June 1871." *Canadian Military History*. Waterloo, ON: Laurier Centre for Military Strategic and Disarmament Studies, 2003.

"Recovery of Bodies Lost on the Yacht *Foam*." *New York Times*, July 22, 1874.

Savoie, John. *Shadows of Niagara*. Niagara Falls, ON: self-published, 2005.

Smith, Barbara. *Ontario Ghost Stories*. Edmonton: Lone Pine, 1998.

————. *Ontario Ghost Stories: Volume II*. Edmonton: Lone Pine, 2002.

Swiggett, Howard. *War Out of Niagara: Walter Butler and the Tory Rangers*. Cranbury, NJ: Scholar's Bookshelf, 2005.

Upton, Kyle. *Niagara's Ghosts 2*. Niagara-on-the-Lake: self-published, 2004.

Willson, Jared. "A Rifleman of Queenston." *Publications of the Buffalo Historical Society* 9 (1906): 373–76.

IMAGE CREDITS

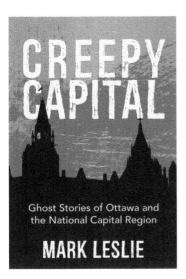

Creepy Capital
Mark Leslie

Come along with paranormal raconteur Mark Leslie as he uncovers first-person accounts of ghostly happenings throughout Ottawa and the surrounding towns — the whole region is rife with ghostly encounters and creepy locales.

Discover the doomed financier who may be haunting the Château Laurier. Experience the eerie shadows and sounds at the Bytown Museum. Listen to the echoing howls of former prison inmates at the Nicholas St. Hostel. And feel the bitter sadness of the ghost of Watson's Mill in Manotick. You'll marvel at the multitude of ghosts that walk the streets and historic landmarks of Canada's capital.

BOOK CREDITS

Acquiring Editor: Margaret Bryant
Editor: Rachel Spence
Proofreader: Jessica Rose

Cover Designer: Laura Boyle
Interior Designer: Lorena Gonzalez Guillen
E-Book Designer: Carmen Giraudy

Publicist: Michelle Melski

DUNDURN

Publisher: J. Kirk Howard
Vice-President: Carl A. Brand
Managing Editor: Kathryn Lane
Director of Design and Production: Jennifer Gallinger
Marketing Manager: Kate Condon-Moriarty
Sales Manager: Synora Van Drine
Publicity Manager: Michelle Melski

Editorial: Allison Hirst, Dominic Farrell, Jenny McWha, Rachel Spence, Elena Radic
Design and Production: Laura Boyle, Carmen Giraudy, Lorena Gonzalez Guillen
Marketing and Publicity: Kendra Martin, Kathryn Bassett

dundurn.com   dundurnpress
@dundurnpress   dundurnpress
dundurnpress   info@dundurn.com

FIND US ON NETGALLEY & GOODREADS TOO!

DUNDURN